Celebrating Sunday for Catholic Families

2019–2020

Kara O'Malley

LITURGY
TRAINING
PUBLICATIONS

Nihil Obstat
Rev. Mr. Daniel G. Welter, JD
Chancellor
Archdiocese of Chicago
August 17, 2018

Imprimatur
Most Rev. Ronald A. Hicks
Vicar General
Archdiocese of Chicago
August 17, 2018

The *Nihil Obstat* and *Imprimatur* are declarations that the material is free from doctrinal or moral error, and thus is granted permission to publish in accordance with c. 827. No legal responsibility is assumed by the grant of this permission. No implication is contained herein that those who have granted the *Nihil Obstat* and *Imprimatur* agree with the content, opinions, or statements expressed.

CELEBRATING SUNDAY FOR CATHOLIC FAMILIES 2019–2020 © 2019 Archdiocese of Chicago: Liturgy Training Publications, 3949 South Racine Avenue, Chicago, IL 60609; 800-933-1800; fax: 800-933-7094; email: orders@ltp.org; website: www.LTP.org. All rights reserved.

This book was edited by Michaela I. Tudela, Víctor R. Pérez was the production editor, Anna Manhart was the designer, and Kari Nicholls was the production artist.

Cover illustration by Eleanor Davis © LTP.

Printed in the United States of America

ISBN 978-1-61671-458-1

CSCF20

"You shall love the LORD your God with all your heart, and with all your soul, and with all your might. Keep these words that I am commanding to you today in your heart. Recite them to your children and talk about them when you are at home and when you are away, when you lie down and when you rise."

(Deuteronomy 6:5–7)

Contents

How to Use

Celebrating Sunday for Catholic Families

This small weekly guide draws on the Gospel for each Sunday and Holyday for the coming year. It is intended to help parents engage their children with the Mass and deepen their appreciation of the richness of their faith life. So often, going to Mass becomes a weekly event that begins and ends at the church door. The brief reflection on an excerpt from the Gospel is intended to spark your thinking about the Scripture that will lead to conversation with your family before and after Mass. Suggestions for questions and conversation starters are provided, as well as some practice or practical way to carry this reflection into the life of the family. Keep in mind, however, that sometimes you may have other needs, concerns, or ideas that are more relevant to your home life at that moment. If so, engage your children with those.

Note that very young children are able to enter into the liturgy through their senses. Singing the hymns, calling their attention to the changing colors of the liturgical seasons, and sitting where they can observe the gestures of the Mass are all ways to form them in the faith. Always remember, as the Rite of Baptism proclaims, you, as parents, are your children's first and most important teachers. We hope that this book will enrich your family's life of faith.

September 8, 2019

Twenty-Third Sunday in Ordinary Time

Hearing the Word

Luke 14:25–33

In the name of the Father, and of the Son, and of the Holy Spirit.

Great crowds were traveling with Jesus, and he turned and addressed them, "If anyone comes to me without hating his father and mother, wife and children, brothers and sisters, and even his own life, he cannot be my disciple. Whoever does not carry his own cross and come after me cannot be my disciple. Which of you wishing to construct a tower does not first sit down and calculate the cost to see if there is enough for its completion? Otherwise, after laying the foundation and finding himself unable to finish the work the onlookers should laugh at him and say, 'This one began to build but did not have the resources to finish.' Or what king marching into battle would not first sit down and decide whether with ten thousand troops he can successfully oppose another king advancing upon him with twenty thousand troops? But if not, while he is still far away, he will send a delegation to ask for peace terms. In the same way, anyone of you who does not renounce all his possessions cannot be my disciple."

Reflecting on the Word

The grace of God is freely given but it is not cheap. Jesus warns his followers to understand fully what the cost of discipleship is before continuing with him, to see with eyes wide open what it means to be a Christian. All of us will encounter different costs as we follow Jesus. Some might lose family or friends. Some will surrender wealth or popularity. Sacrifice is inevitable in the shadow of the cross, but not unbearable. Following Jesus will require commitment. It will require sacrifice. But when we do these, we will open the space in our hearts to receive God's grace.

......ON THE WAY TO MASS

What difficult decisions are you weighing?

ON THE WAY HOME FROM MASS ......

Jesus said that being his disciple would require sacrifice. Think about the choices you might be considering. How would a follower of Jesus choose?

Living the Word

As a family, make a list of the characteristics of Jesus' disciples. Then think about ways you can help one another to be better disciples. What habits have you fallen into as a family that pull you away from Jesus? You might decide to incorporate some new practices (family prayer time, serving at Mass, or volunteering on service projects) that will bring you closer to Jesus.

Twenty-Fourth Sunday in Ordinary Time

Hearing the Word

Luke 15:1–7

In the name of the Father, and of the Son, and of the Holy Spirit.

The tax collectors and sinners were all drawing near to listen to Jesus, but the Pharisees and scribes began to complain, saying, "This man welcomes sinners and eats with them." So to them he addressed this parable. "What man among you having a hundred sheep and losing one of them would not leave the ninety-nine in the desert and go after the lost one until he finds it? And when he does find it, he sets it on his shoulders with great joy and, upon his arrival home, he calls together his friends and neighbors and says to them, 'Rejoice with me because I have found my lost sheep.' I tell you, in just the same way there will be more joy in heaven over one sinner who repents than over ninety-nine righteous people who have no need of repentance."

Reflecting on the Word

In response to the complaints of the Pharisees about his hospitality to sinners, Jesus offers the parable of the lost sheep. God is so loving and understanding and his mercy knows no bounds. He loves those who are already faithful and true, but rejoices when the repentant sinner returns to him.

. . . . . . ON THE WAY TO MASS

We will hear the parable of the lost sheep. If you lost something important to you, what would you do to find it? Would you turn to Jesus to guide you?

ON THE WAY HOME FROM MASS . . . . . .

Do you feel lost sometimes? Do you turn to God for help to repent? What does it mean to forgive those who seek to reconcile with us? How do you show mercy?

Living the Word

The Sacrament of Reconciliation is a joyful one—we are rejoicing in our return to the sheepfold! Take some time this week to rejoice in God's love and mercy. Set aside time for all family members who have been initiated to receive the sacrament. Bring your young children as well; show them where they may sit quietly in the presence of the Blessed Sacrament, and explain that they may pray while they wait.

Afterward, discuss how the sacrament made each of you feel. Talk about how you can share God's love with others.

Twenty-Fifth Sunday in Ordinary Time

Hearing the Word

Luke 16:10–13

In the name of the Father, and of the Son, and of the Holy Spirit.

Jesus said to his disciples, "The person who is trustworthy in very small matters is also trustworthy in great ones; and the person who is dishonest in very small matters is also dishonest in great ones. If, therefore, you are not trustworthy with dishonest wealth, who will trust you with true wealth? If you are not trustworthy with what belongs to another, who will give you what is yours? No servant can serve two masters. He will either hate one and love the other, or be devoted to one and despise the other. You cannot serve both God and mammon."

Reflecting on the Word

A clear line is drawn in today's Gospel: no one can serve two masters. If we love wealth, power, and prestige, then we cannot love God. If we raise wealth and power to the level of a god, and spend our lives in pursuit of it, then we are left with no time or energy to pursue God. If we truly love God, then we must orient our lives toward him and use the resources we have been given for his glory.

·······ON THE WAY TO MASS

If we were very rich and had every material thing we ever needed or wanted, do you think we would still have time for God? Why or why not?

ON THE WAY HOME FROM MASS ·······

What resources has God given to us? How have we shown ourselves to be worthy of his trust?

Living the Word

We are called to be good stewards of the created world, and all the creatures within it. Pope Francis explored this calling in his encyclical, *Laudato Si'*. This week, work on being mindful of all of the resources you consume. Pay attention to how your family can recycle, reuse, and conserve more thoughtfully. Are there any lifestyle changes your family can make to be better stewards of the resources you have been given?

September 29, 2019

Twenty-Sixth Sunday in Ordinary Time

Hearing the Word

Luke 16:19–25

In the name of the Father, and of the Son, and of the Holy Spirit.

Jesus said to the Pharisees, "There was a rich man who dressed in purple garments and fine linen and dined sumptuously each day. And lying at his door was a poor man named Lazarus, covered with sores, who would gladly have eaten his fill of the scraps that fell from the rich man's table. Dogs even used to come and lick his sores. When the poor man died, he was carried away by angels to the bosom of Abraham. The rich man also died and was buried, and from the netherworld, where he was in torment, he raised his eyes and saw Abraham far off and Lazarus at his side. And he cried out, 'Father Abraham, have pity on me. Send Lazarus to dip the tip of his finger in water and cool my tongue, for I am suffering torment in these flames.' Abraham replied, 'My child, remember that you received what was good during your lifetime while Lazarus likewise received what was bad; but now he is comforted here, whereas you are tormented.'"

Reflecting on the Word

St. Augustine described sin as "turning inward" and caring only about the self. In today's Gospel, we see the rich man as a prime example of this sin: a man so selfish that he failed to see someone lying at his door. We are challenged to reflect on the ways in which we turn inward, how we fail to see the needs of those besides ourselves. Our actions have consequences, but so do our lack of actions. God calls us to open our hearts to those in need and to share freely what we have been given.

. . . . . . ON THE WAY TO MASS

Think about times in your life when you have failed to act and help someone. How have you turned inward at the expense of others?

ON THE WAY HOME FROM MASS . . . . . .

How can you share your gifts with others? To whom in your life can you reach out?

Living the Word

This week, reflect as a family on how you can share your wealth and your gifts with others in need. Discuss how you may have failed to act on behalf of others. Make an action plan and follow it. Pray that all of you might turn outward toward God and the people of God.

October 6, 2019

Twenty-Seventh Sunday in Ordinary Time

Hearing the Word

Luke 17:5–10

In the name of the Father, and of the Son, and of the Holy Spirit.

The apostles said to the Lord, "Increase our faith." The Lord replied, "If you have faith the size of a mustard seed, you would say to this mulberry tree, 'Be uprooted and planted in the sea,' and it would obey you.

"Who among you would say to your servant who has just come in from plowing or tending sheep in the field, 'Come here immediately and take your place at the table'? Would he not rather say to him, 'Prepare something for me to eat. Put on your apron and wait on me while I eat and drink. You may eat and drink when I am finished'? Is he grateful to that servant because he did what was commanded? So should it be with you. When you have done all you have been commanded, say, 'We are unprofitable servants; we have done what we were obliged to do.'"

Reflecting on the Word

Jesus' disciples ask for an increase of faith. In response, Jesus tells them this parable, which exhorts us all to fulfill our duties to the master (God) faithfully. Our faith will grow and change through the loving attention to the ordinary tasks of life. These tasks can include our work, our service to our loved ones, our responsibility to our neighbors, and especially the duty of prayer we owe to God. Faith increases in the quiet, routine work of daily life.

······ ON THE WAY TO MASS

What is your daily work? What is your attitude toward this work?

ON THE WAY HOME FROM MASS ······

What does it mean for you to serve God? Do you faithfully undertake the work he has called you to do?

Living the Word

Often we see work as something to endure but not necessarily enjoy. In contrast, St. Dominic Savio said, "Nothing seems tiresome or painful when you are working for a Master who pays well." In what ways has God paid you well for your labor? Ask your children whether their faith is increased by the work they do (chores or job, schoolwork, prayer, athletics or the arts). How do these tasks serve God? Share ways in which you have grown in faith through your own daily work. This week, pray for the intercession of St. Joseph the Worker.

October 13, 2019

Twenty-Eighth Sunday in Ordinary Time

Hearing the Word

Luke 17:11–19

In the name of the Father, and of the Son, and of the Holy Spirit.

As Jesus continued his journey to Jerusalem, he traveled through Samaria and Galilee. As he was entering a village, ten lepers met him. They stood at a distance from him and raised their voice saying, "Jesus, Master! Have pity on us!" And when he saw them, he said, "Go show yourselves to the priests." As they were going they were cleansed. And one of them, realizing he had been healed, returned, glorifying God in a loud voice; and he fell at the feet of Jesus and thanked him. He was a Samaritan. Jesus said in reply, "Ten were cleansed, were they not? Where are the other nine? Has none but this foreigner returned to give thanks to God?" Then he said to him, "Stand up and go; your faith has saved you."

Reflecting on the Word

The ten lepers, in faith, called out to Jesus for mercy, and their faith was rewarded with physical healing. The only one to return to the Lord in gratitude was the Samaritan. His thankfulness for his physical healing leads to his spiritual healing. Through this encounter, Jesus shows us that no one, not a leper or even a Samaritan, is beyond God's mercy. Salvation is offered to each of us if we only cry out for God's mercy and respond to his love with thankfulness and praise.

•••••• ON THE WAY TO MASS

Ask everyone to listen to the Gospel and to the homily. Have them pay attention to parts of the Mass when we pray for those who are suffering or ill.

ON THE WAY HOME FROM MASS ••••••

God does not ignore our cries for help or healing. Do you remember to thank God for his goodness to you? How can you show your gratitude?

Living the Word

The word *Eucharist* means "thanksgiving." How do we thank God in a special way at Mass? Each night this week, set aside time when you can say thank you to God. Have your children name one thing from that day that they are grateful for. In prayer, you might say, "Thank you God for . . ."

Twenty-Ninth Sunday in Ordinary Time

Hearing the Word
Luke 18:1–7

In the name of the Father, and of the Son, and of the Holy Spirit.

Jesus told his disciples a parable about the necessity for them to pray always without becoming weary. He said, "There was a judge in a certain town who neither feared God nor respected any human being. And a widow in that town used to come to him and say, 'Render a just decision for me against my adversary.' For a long time the judge was unwilling, but eventually he thought, 'While it is true that I neither fear God nor respect any human being, because this widow keeps bothering me I shall deliver a just decision for her lest she finally come and strike me.'" The Lord said, "Pay attention to what the dishonest judge says. Will not God then secure the rights of his chosen ones who call out to him day and night? Will he be slow to answer them?"

Reflecting on the Word

Today's Gospel parable is about persistence in prayer. Jesus teaches us that we must pray constantly and not become tired of doing so. Prayer is one way we may deepen our faith and become stronger.

...... ON THE WAY TO MASS

What does prayer mean to you? Why do you pray?

ON THE WAY HOME FROM MASS ......

Reflect on the widow from the Gospel. Why do you think she kept bothering the judge? What might have given her strength to persist in her request? What does this teach us about praying to God?

Living the Word

The Our Father is a prayer that Jesus himself taught us to pray. Challenge your family this week to pray the Our Father every day. Help your younger children learn the prayer, and go over the meaning of certain words and phrases. Pray unceasingly.

Thirtieth Sunday in Ordinary Time

Hearing the Word

Luke 18:9–14

In the name of the Father, and of the Son, and of the Holy Spirit.

Jesus addressed this parable to those who were convinced of their own righteousness and despised everyone else. "Two people went up to the temple area to pray; one was a Pharisee and the other was a tax collector. The Pharisee took up his position and spoke this prayer to himself, 'O God, I thank you that I am not like the rest of humanity— greedy, dishonest, adulterous—or even like this tax collector. I fast twice a week, and I pay tithes on my whole income.' But the tax collector stood off at a distance and would not even raise his eyes to heaven but beat his breast and prayed, 'O God, be merciful to me a sinner.' I tell you, the latter went home justified, not the former; for whoever exalts himself will be humbled, and the one who humbles himself will be exalted."

Reflecting on the Word

This week we continue our focus on prayer. It is human nature to compare ourselves to others. It is easier to focus on the ways in which we are "better" than others than to attend to our own failings. In fixating on the faults of others, the Pharisee blinds himself to his own sins and they become obstacles to his relationship with God. The tax collector, in contrast, confesses his sins and begs the mercy of God. He approaches God with fear and trembling, fully aware of his own failures, and God will exalt him in return.

• • • • • • ON THE WAY TO MASS

This week's Gospel reading will teach us more about prayer. Ask your children to pay attention to the words and actions of the Pharisee and tax collector.

ON THE WAY HOME FROM MASS • • • • • •

Have your children explain the difference between the Pharisee and the tax collector. Discuss why Jesus preferred the prayer of the tax collector when the Pharisee was indeed trying to be good and follow the rules.

Living the Word

Explore the virtue of humility as a family. Ask your children how Jesus showed humility in his earthly life, and find stories of Jesus and the saints practicing humility. Discuss how the path to holiness looks different for different people. Why should we avoid comparing ourselves to others? How can comparisons be an obstacle to holiness?

Solemnity of All Saints

Hearing the Word
Matthew 5:3–12a

In the name of the Father, and of the Son, and of the Holy Spirit.

[Jesus said]: "Blessed are the poor in spirit, / for theirs is the Kingdom of heaven. / Blessed are they who mourn, / for they will be comforted. / Blessed are the meek, / for they will inherit the land. / Blessed are they who hunger and thirst for righteousness, / for they will be satisfied. / Blessed are the merciful, / for they will be shown mercy. / Blessed are the clean of heart, / for they will see God. / Blessed are the peacemakers, / for they will be called children of God. / Blessed are they who are persecuted for the sake of righteousness, / for theirs is the Kingdom of heaven. / Blessed are you when they insult you and persecute you / and utter every kind of evil against you falsely because of me. / Rejoice and be glad, / for your reward will be great in heaven."

Reflecting on the Word

Today we honor all those who have found eternal happiness with God. All of the saints, both those canonized and the many more still unrecognized here on earth, sought and lived holy lives. The saints are the embodiment of the Beatitudes. As such, they demonstrated humility and forgiveness, purity of heart, a thirst for justice and peace, though they were persecuted in the name of their faith. On this solemnity, we also joyfully celebrate our own vocation to become saints and follow in their holy footsteps.

•••••• ON THE WAY TO MASS

Why is it helpful to have good role models in our lives?

ON THE WAY HOME FROM MASS ••••••

Which Beatitude can we try to live out now?

Living the Word

In the Beatitudes, Jesus teaches us that to be blessed means to be vulnerable, to rely on God. We must give up the do-it-yourself attitude toward life and trust in God. Immerse your family in the lives of the saints this week. Read (or act out) stories of saints who are special to your family and discuss how they lived the Beatitudes. What qualities do you most admire in them? Pray that you might all become saints.

On November 2, we celebrate All Souls' Day, or the Commemoration of All the Faithful Departed. Share stories about them with your family; show photos if you have them.

Thirty-First Sunday in Ordinary Time

Hearing the Word

Luke 19:1–10

In the name of the Father, and of the Son, and of the Holy Spirit.

At that time, Jesus came to Jericho and intended to pass through the town. Now a man there named Zacchaeus, who was a chief tax collector and also a wealthy man, was seeking to see who Jesus was; but he could not see him because of the crowd, for he was short in stature. So he ran ahead and climbed a sycamore tree in order to see Jesus, who was about to pass that way. When he reached the place, Jesus looked up and said to him, "Zacchaeus, come down quickly, for today I must stay at your house." And he came down quickly and received him with joy. When they all saw this, they began to grumble, saying, "He has gone to stay at the house of a sinner." But Zacchaeus stood there and said to the Lord, "Behold, half of my possessions, Lord, I shall give to the poor, and if I have extorted anything from anyone I shall repay it four times over." And Jesus said to him, "Today salvation has come to this house because this man too is a descendant of Abraham. For the Son of Man has come to seek and to save what was lost."

Reflecting on the Word

Zacchaeus went "seeking to see who Jesus was." He found himself captivated by Jesus: first, to go so far as to climb a tree just to see him, then to welcome Jesus in his home, and finally to give up half his possessions to the poor and repay others four times what he extorted from them. Because of that encounter with Jesus, Zacchaeus changes.

•••••• ON THE WAY TO MASS

Ask your children to pay attention to the story of Zacchaeus and the change that happens when Jesus enters his life.

ON THE WAY HOME FROM MASS ••••••

Do we encounter Jesus in our lives? When do we notice God's presence? Do we welcome him in our hearts? Are our lives a reflection of Christian values?

Living the Word

Go to ZacchaeusHouse.org (or find Zacchaeus House on social media) to learn more about this home for men who need shelter and healing. Residents can live at Zacchaeus House while they work toward independent living by finding jobs, learning trades, or going back to school. Peruse the photos of those who volunteer their time and treasure, as well as of the men who have been helped. Look at the list of needs, and as a family, decide how you can help.

Thirty-Second Sunday in Ordinary Time

Hearing the Word

Luke 20:34–38

In the name of the Father, and of the Son, and of the Holy Spirit.

Jesus said to [the Sadducees], "The children of this age marry and are given in marriage; but those who are deemed worthy to attain to the coming age and to the resurrection of the dead neither marry nor are given in marriage. They can no longer die, for they are like angels; and they are the children of God because they are the ones who will rise. That the dead will rise even Moses made known in the passage about the bush, when he called 'Lord,' the God of Abraham, the God of Isaac, and the God of Jacob; and he is not God of the dead, but of the living, for to him all are alive."

Reflecting on the Word

The Sadducees had approached Jesus, looking to trick him with a question of which man, in the resurrection, will be married to a woman widowed seven times. Jesus does not respond directly to their query. Instead, he says that to God, all are alive—even the dead. Our Catholic funeral liturgy tells us that life is changed, not ended. Though relationships may cease after death, the love that formed them will not. Love never dies, and we are destined to live in that Love—that is, to live in God—forever.

•••••• ON THE WAY TO MASS

What do you think heaven is like? What will it be like to be with God forever?

ON THE WAY HOME FROM MASS ••••••

Children have questions about death and the afterlife. Explain that your departed loved one is at peace; that their soul is alive and with God. Encourage your children to share feelings or fears.

Living the Word

In the Catholic tradition, November is a time to honor the dead. Set up a prayer table devoted to your beloved dead. Add a candle, flowers, Bible, and photographs or other mementos. Pray that all of your beloved dead might be with God in heaven, and give thanks for the love you still share with them. Invite your children to draw or write about a memory they have about the departed loved one, and talk about why that person was special to them.

November 17, 2019

Thirty-Third Sunday in Ordinary Time

Hearing the Word

Luke 21:5–11

In the name of the Father, and of the Son, and of the Holy Spirit.

While some people were speaking about how the temple was adorned with costly stones and votive offerings, Jesus said, "All that you see here—the days will come when there will not be left a stone upon another stone that will not be thrown down."

Then they asked him, "Teacher, when will this happen? And what sign will there be when all these things are about to happen?" He answered, "See that you not be deceived, for many will come in my name, saying, 'I am he,' and 'The time has come.' Do not follow them! When you hear of wars and insurrections, do not be terrified; for such things must happen first, but it will not immediately be the end." Then he said to them, "Nation will rise against nation, and kingdom against kingdom. There will be powerful earthquakes, famines, and plagues from place to place; and awesome sights and mighty signs will come from the sky."

Reflecting on the Word

As the liturgical year wanes, our readings at Mass focus on the end times. This week, we hear Jesus predict the destruction of the Temple of Jerusalem, an unfathomable prospect to his listeners. Jesus warns them (and us) that even in the face of much destruction and evil, they should not give in to terror. We must remain strong and steadfast, hoping in God and working for good. Though life may seem terrible and hopeless at times, God's morning light will overtake the darkness of night.

......ON THE WAY TO MASS

Have you ever been terrified? How did you overcome the terror?

ON THE WAY HOME FROM MASS ......

What does it mean to hope in God? Why is this hope so important? Talk about how faith helps us to respond to worries, fears, and crises.

Living the Word

We hear a lot about terror in our world today, and sometimes it seems that our societal problems are too great and cannot improve. But because we hope in God, we are called to tirelessly bring light to the dark places of the world. Learn more about who is working in your community or in the wider global society to combat terror or destruction. Pray for this person or organization this week, and make a plan for how your family can support and contribute to their mission.

Next Sunday is the last in our liturgical year. We will celebrate a new one on the First Sunday of Advent.

Solemnity of Our Lord Jesus Christ, King of the Universe

Hearing the Word

Luke 23:35–43

In the name of the Father, and of the Son, and of the Holy Spirit.

The rulers sneered at Jesus and said, "He saved others, let him save himself if he is the chosen one, the Christ of God." Even the soldiers jeered at him. As they approached to offer him wine they called out, "If you are King of the Jews, save yourself." Above him there was an inscription that read, "This is the King of the Jews."

Now one of the criminals hanging there reviled Jesus, saying, "Are you not the Christ? Save yourself and us." The other, however, rebuking him, said in reply, "Have you no fear of God, for you are subject to the same condemnation? And indeed, we have been condemned justly, for the sentence we received corresponds to our crimes, but this man has done nothing criminal." Then he said, "Jesus, remember me when you come into your kingdom." He replied to him, "Amen, I say to you, today you will be with me in Paradise."

Reflecting on the Word

Jesus Christ is a strange kind of king. He was born into poverty and lived simply. He had followers but no army to assert his power. He had no palace, no possessions, nothing to signal his rank to others. In the end, he was crucified like a common criminal, and those gathered around the cross mocked his claim to kingship. But the criminal suffering alongside him saw Christ clearly: strength in humility, power in sacrifice. This man enjoined Jesus to remember him. May we have the clarity to do the same.

......ON THE WAY TO MASS

How would you describe a king?

ON THE WAY HOME FROM MASS ......

Explain to your children that today we celebrate the Solemnity of Our Lord Jesus Christ, King of the Universe. This is an awe-inspiring title. What kind of king is Jesus? How is he different from kings and rulers of the world?

Living the Word

We are called to act mercifully toward others, the earth, the universe, and ourselves. The more we act with mercy toward all of creation, the more mercy will become a grace deeply embedded in our spiritual lives. Others may then witness God's mercy in the way we care for those on the margins and in our care for creation. This Thursday, Americans will be celebrating Thanksgiving Day. We will be preparing our homes and welcoming guests. We also need to prepare our hearts to welcome Christ the King. Thank God for abundant blessings.

December 1, 2019

First Sunday of Advent

Hearing the Word
Matthew 24:37–42

In the name of the Father, and of the Son, and of the Holy Spirit.

Jesus said to his disciples, "For as it was in the days of Noah, so it will be at the coming of the Son of Man. In those days before the flood, they were eating and drinking, marrying and giving in marriage, up to the day that Noah entered the ark. They did not know until the flood came and carried them all away. So will it be also at the coming of the Son of Man. Two men will be out in the field; one will be taken, and one will be left. Two women will be grinding at the mill; one will be taken, and one will be left. Therefore, stay awake! For you do not know on which day your Lord will come. Be sure of this: if the master of the house had known the hour of night when the thief was coming, he would have stayed awake and not let his house be broken into. So too, you also must be prepared, for at an hour you do not expect, the Son of Man will come."

Reflecting on the Word

In Advent, we wait. We wait for the coming of Jesus—in that stable in Bethlehem, in our hearts, and at the end of all things. Our wait should not be characterized only by Christmas shopping, parties, or gift wrapping. It should also be marked by prayer, service, and repentance. We wait in hope for the Lord to come, knowing that he will come "at an hour you do not expect." Stay awake! Don't ignore God. Let us open our hearts to the possibilities of renewal and generously welcome the Lord into our lives.

•••••• ON THE WAY TO MASS

Alert your children to the start of a new liturgical year. Ask them to notice what new color they see and changes in the church environment.

ON THE WAY HOME FROM MASS ••••••

Talk about how your family can actively wait for Jesus this Advent season. Some ideas could be regular family prayer, service to the community, or an Advent calendar with daily acts of love.

Living the Word

For family prayer, light an Advent wreath (or any candles) and listen to the Taizé chant "Wait for the Lord." (Find recordings online.) Sing along once you are comfortable with the refrain. Even if the world rushes toward Christmas Day, use this time to focus purposefully on Christ to come into our hearts and lives.

December 8, 2019

Second Sunday of Advent

Hearing the Word

Matthew 3:1–6

In the name of the Father, and of the Son, and of the Holy Spirit.

John the Baptist appeared, preaching in the desert of Judea and saying, "Repent, for the kingdom of heaven is at hand!" It was of him that the prophet Isaiah had spoken when he said: / *A voice of one crying out in the desert, / Prepare the way of the Lord, / make straight his paths. /* John wore clothing made of camel's hair and had a leather belt around his waist. His food was locusts and wild honey. At that time Jerusalem, all Judea, and the whole region around the Jordan were going out to him and were being baptized by him in the Jordan River as they acknowledged their sins.

Reflecting on the Word

All of us want to be prepared. We prepare for bad weather, medical emergencies, tests, job interviews, new babies, or first days of school. In most of these cases, our preparations include having proper supplies and a plan of action. John the Baptist preaches a different kind of preparation: the preparation of the heart. As Christians, we must be constantly vigilant and repentant, keeping our hearts pure and holy, for the Kingdom of Heaven is at hand.

•••••• ON THE WAY TO MASS

Do your children know who John the Baptist is? He was the cousin of Jesus. Elizabeth, his mother, was the cousin of Mary. Tell your children the story of the Visitation and of the baby John leaping in his mother's womb.

ON THE WAY HOME FROM MASS ••••••

Talk about John's exhortation for the people to repent, for the Kingdom of God is at hand. Explain to your children that John was telling people to turn their lives around in preparation for Jesus' coming.

Living the Word

Prepare your hearts for the Lord's coming by participating in a parish reconciliation service or going to confession at your church. At home, have your children draw a picture of a path they are traveling to Jesus. What gets in between them and Jesus? Ask them to keep this obstacle in mind as they receive the sacrament.

December 15, 2019

THIRD SUNDAY OF ADVENT

Hearing the Word

Matthew 11:2–6

In the name of the Father, and of the Son, and of the Holy Spirit.

When John the Baptist heard in prison of the works of the Messiah, he sent his disciples to Jesus with this question, "Are you the one who is to come, or should we look for another?" Jesus said to them in reply, "Go and tell John what you hear and see: the blind regain their sight, the lame walk, lepers are cleansed, the deaf hear, the dead are raised, and the poor have the good news proclaimed to them. And blessed is the one who takes no offense at me."

Reflecting on the Word

John the Baptist has expectations of the Messiah. We, too, have expectations of God. What were John and his disciples expecting? Rather than telling them directly that he was the Messiah, Jesus asks them to look at all who have been restored and healed. This is indeed cause for rejoicing at the coming of the Savior.

• • • • • • ON THE WAY TO MASS

Today is the Third Sunday of Advent, or Gaudete Sunday. The Latin word *gaudete* means "rejoice." Ask your family to notice the color rose in the liturgical environment. Why is this color used today?

ON THE WAY HOME FROM MASS • • • • • •

What were the people of God looking for in a Messiah? What did they find instead? What are your expectations of God?

Living the Word

Have you ever unexpectedly encountered God? Tell your children about it. Ask them also to share moments when they personally encountered God, or when they met him in unexpected ways.

Fourth Sunday of Advent

Hearing the Word
Matthew 1:18–24

In the name of the Father, and of the Son, and of the Holy Spirit.

This is how the birth of Jesus Christ came about. When his mother Mary was betrothed to Joseph, but before they lived together, she was found with child through the holy Spirit. Joseph her husband, since he was a righteous man, yet unwilling to expose her to shame, decided to divorce her quietly. Such was his intention when, behold, the angel of the Lord appeared to him in a dream and said, "Joseph, son of David, do not be afraid to take Mary your wife into your home. For it is through the Holy Spirit that this child has been conceived in her. She will bear a son and you are to name him Jesus, because he will save his people from their sins." All this took place to fulfill what the Lord had said through the prophet: *Behold, the virgin shall be with child and bear a son, / and they shall name him Emmanuel, /* which means "God is with us." When Joseph awoke, he did as the angel of the Lord had commanded him and took his wife into his home.

Reflecting on the Word

Today we hear the central message of Advent: "God is with us." Mary was afraid when the angel Gabriel revealed that she had been chosen by God to bear his son. Joseph was perturbed when Mary was found to be pregnant, for he was a righteous man. Yet, because they both, in faith, said yes to the call of God, God was with them in a deeply personal and miraculous way. Likewise, we have each been called and chosen to make the light of Christ shine in the dark places of the world.

· · · · · · ON THE WAY TO MASS

Though Christmas is very close, it is still Advent. How is your family doing with your Advent preparations?

ON THE WAY HOME FROM MASS · · · · · ·

Think about how courageous Mary and Joseph were to say yes to God, and how they demonstrated great faith by responding affirmatively. Have you ever said yes to God even though you felt scared or nervous?

Living the Word

Immerse yourself in the experience of the Holy Family and the events of Jesus' conception and birth. Read all or parts of the infancy narrative according to Luke (1:5—2:52). Consider participating in a celebration of Las Posadas in your area. Discuss how Joseph and Mary must have been feeling as the birth of Jesus approached, and pray that Jesus might find a home in your family in the coming year.

December 25, 2019

Solemnity of the Nativity of the Lord (Mass during the Night)

Hearing the Word

Luke 2:1–7a, 8–14

In the name of the Father, and of the Son, and of the Holy Spirit.

In those days a decree went out from Caesar Augustus that the whole world should be enrolled. This was the first enrollment, when Quirinius was governor of Syria. So all went to be enrolled, each to his own town. And Joseph too went up from Galilee from the town of Nazareth to Judea, to the city of David that is called Bethlehem, because he was of the house and family of David, to be enrolled with Mary, his betrothed, who was with child. While they were there, the time came for her to have her child, and she gave birth to her firstborn son.

Now there were shepherds in that region living in the fields and keeping the night watch over their flock. The angel of the Lord appeared to them and the glory of the Lord shone around them, and they were struck with great fear. The angel said to them, "Do not be afraid; for behold, I proclaim to you good news of great joy that will be for all the people.

For today in the city of David a savior has been born for you who is Christ and Lord. And this will be a sign for you: you will find an infant wrapped in swaddling clothes and lying in a manger." And suddenly there was a multitude of the heavenly host with the angel, praising God and saying: / "Glory to God in the highest / and on earth peace to those on whom his favor rests."

Reflecting on the Word

The glory of the Lord shone around them. The shepherds were going about their daily life, tending the sheep, when they were suddenly surrounded by the glory of the Lord. The whole world is wrapped in glory. Two millennia ago, as well as today, the Word of God is born, the eternal Lord lowered himself to enter into human life. With the angels, we proclaim this news of great joy: God has become man, and has filled humanity with his glory. *Glory to God in the highest!*

......ON THE WAY TO MASS

Ask your children to listen closely to tonight's Gospel. How can we also show our joy and gratitude for Jesus' birth?

ON THE WAY HOME FROM MASS ......

What changes did you notice in church?

Living the Word

Christmas is a major feast, and the celebration lasts for more than just a day! It continues for an octave, or eight days, ending with the Solemnity of Mary, the Holy Mother of God, on January 1. In the Church's liturgy, each day of the Christmas octave is a new Christmas—we pray the same prayers as on December 25 and sing the Gloria every day at Mass. Keep the celebration going at home as well! Do special, fun activities as a family, and invite friends and family over for celebratory meals all week.

Feast of the Holy Family of Jesus, Mary, and Joseph

Hearing the Word
Matthew 2:19–23

In the name of the Father, and of the Son, and of the Holy Spirit.

When Herod had died, behold, the angel of the Lord appeared in a dream to Joseph in Egypt and said, "Rise, take the child and his mother and go to the land of Israel, for those who sought the child's life are dead." He rose, took the child and his mother, and went to the land of Israel. But when he heard that Archelaus was ruling over Judea in place of his father Herod, he was afraid to go back there. And because he had been warned in a dream, he departed for the region of Galilee. He went and dwelt in a town called Nazareth, so that what had been spoken through the prophets might be fulfilled, *"He shall be called a Nazorean."*

Reflecting on the Word

The Holy Family was rooted in fidelity to God. They faithfully followed his command to flee to Egypt and then to return after Herod had died. They went to a foreign country, leaving family, friends, and livelihood, without knowing what the outcome would be. In the quiet simplicity of the Nazareth household, the child Jesus learned about virtue, obedience, and holiness from his parents. The Holy Family is an icon of family life: a life built upon faith, fidelity, and love.

......ON THE WAY TO MASS

Explain to your children what today's feast is about. What are some of your family's qualities?

ON THE WAY HOME FROM MASS ......

Refer to the list of qualities that describe your family. What do you have in common with the Holy Family?

Living the Word

To celebrate this feast, plan a fun family day. Visit a museum, go sledding or ice skating, or do some other family activity. Finish the day by preparing a special meal: let each family member choose one food item for the meal. For prayer that evening, have each member of the family light a candle (baptismal candles would be especially appropriate), and pray that the flame of faith may be strengthened for each of you.

Solemnity of Mary, the Holy Mother of God

Hearing the Word

Luke 2:16–21

In the name of the Father, and of the Son, and of the Holy Spirit.

The shepherds went in haste to Bethlehem and found Mary and Joseph, and the infant lying in the manger. When they saw this, they made known the message that had been told them about this child. All who heard it were amazed by what had been told them by the shepherds. And Mary kept all these things, reflecting on them in her heart. Then the shepherds returned, glorifying and praising God for all they had heard and seen, just as it had been told to them.

When eight days were completed for his circumcision, he was named Jesus, the name given him by the angel before he was conceived in the womb.

Reflecting on the Word

Mary is the Mother of God. She felt the Creator of the world stir in her womb, and nursed the King of Kings at her breast. She sang the Word made flesh to sleep, and soothed the hurts of the Prince of Peace. And she kept all these ordinary, miraculous moments, reflecting on them in her heart. All those at the manger were amazed at the angels' word: that this tiny babe was Christ and Lord. Today we marvel that this Son of God is also the son of Mary, that she said yes to the miracle of daily life with God.

......ON THE WAY TO MASS

We call Mary the Mother of the Church. What does this mean to you?

ON THE WAY HOME FROM MASS ......

An important aspect of the spiritual life is listening to and reflecting on Scripture. Travel home in silence today. Ask your children to think about how they will resolve to spend more time with God this year.

Living the Word

As you embark on a new year as a family, discuss how you may grow in faith in the coming year. Are there any commitments to service or prayer that your family can take on in the new year? How can you help one another? How can you help others in your community or the wider world? Include your resolutions in your prayer space so you can be reminded of them throughout the year.

January 5, 2020

Solemnity of the Epiphany of the Lord

Hearing the Word
Matthew 2:1–5, 7–11

In the name of the Father, and of the Son, and of the Holy Spirit.

When Jesus was born in Bethlehem of Judea, in the days of King Herod, behold, magi from the east arrived in Jerusalem, saying, "Where is the newborn king of the Jews? We saw his star at its rising and have come to do him homage." When King Herod heard this, he was greatly troubled, and all Jerusalem with him. Assembling all the chief priests and the scribes of the people, he inquired of them where the Christ was to be born. They said to him, "In Bethlehem of Judea . . ." Then Herod called the magi secretly and ascertained from them the time of the star's appearance. He sent them to Bethlehem and said, "Go and search diligently for the child. When you have found him, bring me word, that I too may go and do him homage." After their audience with the king they set out. And behold, the star that they had seen at its rising preceded them, until it came and stopped over the place where the child was. They were overjoyed at seeing the star, and on entering the house they saw the child with Mary his mother. They prostrated themselves and did him homage. Then they opened their treasures and offered him gifts of gold, frankincense, and myrrh.

Reflecting on the Word

Matthew's account is the only one to describe the visit of the Magi. The journey of the Magi revealed the significance of Jesus' birth. *Epiphany* means "revelation": the star revealed the way to Jesus, and their gifts to the newborn revealed his true identity (his royalty, divinity, and eventual death). We all experience moments of epiphany: moments when the darkness is dispelled and we see the world in a new way, moments when we find the courage to travel outside the safe borders of our normal lives. On this feast, consider where the star is leading you. How is Christ being revealed in your life?

• • • • • • ON THE WAY TO MASS

The Magi brought gifts to Jesus. What gifts do each of you bring?

ON THE WAY HOME FROM MASS • • • • • •

What epiphanies or revelations have you experienced? How was God present?

Living the Word

Perform the traditional "chalking the door" at your home. Use chalk to write the following above the entrance of your home: 20 + C + M + B + 20. The letters have two meanings: they are the initials of the Magi's names—Caspar, Melchior, and Balthasar—and they also abbreviate the Latin phrase *Christus mansionem benedicat* ("May Christ bless the house"). The + signs represent the cross, and the year is written at either end. This inscription is a prayer that Christ bless the home and stay with those who dwell therein throughout the entire year.

Feast of the Baptism of the Lord

Hearing the Word

Matthew 3:13–17

In the name of the Father, and of the Son, and of the Holy Spirit.

Jesus came from Galilee to John at the Jordan to be baptized by him. John tried to prevent him, saying, "I need to be baptized by you, and yet you are coming to me?" Jesus said to him in reply, "Allow it now, for thus it is fitting for us to fulfill all righteousness." Then he allowed him. After Jesus was baptized, he came up from the water and behold, the heavens were opened for him, and he saw the Spirit of God descending like a dove and coming upon him. And a voice came from the heavens, saying, "This is my beloved Son, with whom I am well pleased."

Reflecting on the Word

The baptism of Jesus is another epiphany, a moment of revelation. In this baptism, the Trinity is revealed (the voice of God the Father, the person of Jesus Christ, and the dove). Jesus' baptism opens the door for all of us to participate in the life of God. We have been called to the same baptismal waters. In Baptism, we receive a new life in Christ—we put on Christ, like a garment—and are made into sons and daughters of God, in whom he is well pleased.

......ON THE WAY TO MASS

Do you see yourself as a beloved child of God?

ON THE WAY HOME FROM MASS ......

What can we learn about the life of the Trinity from the baptism of Jesus?

Living the Word

Share memories of your family members' Baptisms. Show pictures or videos, candles and baptismal garments. Ask your children what they think it means to be a son or daughter of God. Add an icon of the baptism of Jesus to your prayer table. (Use the keywords "religious icon" and "baptism of Jesus" to search for icons to purchase online.) Read this Gospel again as the family looks upon the image and discuss how Father, Son, and Holy Spirit are represented.

January 19, 2020

Second Sunday in Ordinary Time

Hearing the Word

John 1:29–34

In the name of the Father, and of the Son, and of the Holy Spirit.

John the Baptist saw Jesus coming toward him and said, "Behold, the Lamb of God, who takes away the sin of the world. He is the one of whom I said, 'A man is coming after me who ranks ahead of me because he existed before me.' I did not know him, but the reason why I came baptizing with water was that he might be made known to Israel." John testified further, saying, "I saw the Spirit come down like a dove from the sky and remain upon him. I did not know him, but the one who sent me to baptize with water told me, 'On whomever you see the Spirit come down and remain, he is the one who will baptize with the Holy Spirit.' Now I have seen and testified that he is the Son of God."

Reflecting on the Word

John the Baptist had already given up all that he owned, travelling around and preaching repentance of sins. This day, when he was surrounded by his followers (the fruit of his work and sacrifice) he looked toward Jesus and sent them all to follow Jesus. John showed great humility as a witness to Christ, giving up every remnant of his accomplishments in service of God. Like John, it is our call to direct our successes, achievements, and glory back to God, that we may make him known in all we do.

• • • • • • ON THE WAY TO MASS

How would you respond if someone asked you, "Whose disciple are you?"

ON THE WAY HOME FROM MASS • • • • • •

John the Baptist was Jesus' cousin, and undoubtedly knew him his whole life. He knew that Jesus was the Son of God, the Messiah that the people had been waiting for. Explain to your children that we recognize God's presence, too: at the Mass, he is present in the Word, in the Eucharist, and in the worshipping assembly.

Living the Word

The saints all witnessed to the glory and love of God by their lives. Like John, their words and actions were directed to give glory to God. Look at the lives of two or three of your favorite saints. How did they witness to God? How did their lives give glory to God? Discuss some ways you can witness to God's love in your daily life.

January 26, 2020

Third Sunday in Ordinary Time

Hearing the Word

Matthew 4:13–17

In the name of the Father, and of the Son, and of the Holy Spirit.

[Jesus] left Nazareth and went to live in Capernaum by the sea, in the region of Zebulun and Naphtali, that what had been said through Isaiah the prophet might be fulfilled: / *Land of Zebulun and land of Naphtali, / the way to the sea, beyond the Jordan, / Galilee of the Gentiles, / the people who sit in darkness have seen a great light, / on those dwelling in a land overshadowed by death / light has arisen.* / From that time on, Jesus began to preach and say, "Repent, for the kingdom of heaven is at hand."

Reflecting on the Word

During the winter in North America, the days are short and the hours in the dark are long. The world is full of suffering and death, wars and famines, poverty and addiction, violence and despair. It is easy to feel worn down by the darkness. But the light of God dawned upon the world at the darkest time of year. Light and life and hope have arisen. Our hope was born in Bethlehem and he is still being born in our hearts and in our lives, bringing light to dark places.

• • • • • • ON THE WAY TO MASS

Talk about various examples of light. What does light do for us? How might life be like if we did not have light?

ON THE WAY HOME FROM MASS • • • • • •

What are you struggling with right now in your life? How has Jesus been a light in your life? What does hope in Jesus mean to you?

Living the Word

If possible, attend an evening prayer (vespers) service at church, a seminary, a convent or monastery. Or, pray vespers at home as a family. You can find the prayers of the day at www.iBreviary.org. Light candles to invoke a sense of reverence to your celebration. After your celebration of evening prayer, talk about the experience. What does it mean to say that Jesus is the Light of the World? What are some ways that you can bring light to the dark places of the world?

February 2, 2020

Feast of the Presentation of the Lord

Hearing the Word

Luke 2:25–32

In the name of the Father, and of the Son, and of the Holy Spirit.

Now there was a man in Jerusalem whose name was Simeon. This man was righteous and devout, awaiting the consolation of Israel, and the Holy Spirit was upon him. It had been revealed to him by the Holy Spirit that he should not see death before he had seen the Christ of the Lord. He came in the Spirit into the temple; and when the parents brought in the child Jesus to perform the custom of the law in regard to him, he took him into his arms and blessed God saying: / "Now, Master, you may let your servant go / in peace, according to your word, / for my eyes have seen your salvation, /which you prepared in sight of all the peoples / a light for revelation to the Gentiles, / and glory for your people Israel."

Reflecting on the Word

Simeon speaks of the longing in all human hearts. As St. Augustine expressed it, "Our hearts are restless until they rest in [God]." Upon setting eyes on the infant Jesus, Simeon's longing is put to rest. He saw the Light, Jesus Christ, and saw everything about his life, the world, and his destiny. So, too, is it our destiny to meet God face to face, to look into the Light, which illumines every darkness of sin and fear and death. In God, we find the peace that the world cannot provide.

......ON THE WAY TO MASS

Ask your children to listen for more references to light. Why is the idea of light significant?

ON THE WAY HOME FROM MASS ......

How was Simeon changed by his encounter with the baby Jesus? Have you ever been changed by an encounter with God?

Living the Word

This feast is also commonly known as Candlemas (since Jesus is called a "light for revelation"). Many churches offer a blessing of candles, including those to be used in prayer at home. On the evening of the feast, hold a candlelit procession around your house, and conclude by praying the Canticle of Simeon (*Nunc Dimittis*) found in this Gospel reading.

February 9, 2020

Fifth Sunday in Ordinary Time

Hearing the Word

Matthew 5:13–16

In the name of the Father, and of the Son, and of the Holy Spirit.

Jesus said to his disciples: "You are the salt of the earth. But if salt loses its taste, with what can it be seasoned? It is no longer good for anything but to be thrown out and trampled underfoot. You are the light of the world. A city set on a mountain cannot be hidden. Nor do they light a lamp and then put it under a bushel basket; it is set on a lampstand, where it gives light to all in the house. Just so, your light must shine before others, that they may see your good deeds and glorify your heavenly Father."

Reflecting on the Word

Jesus uses the familiar metaphors of salt and light to describe the life of discipleship. We are the light of the world. It is our work to shine before others, that they might know and glorify God. Our lives are the light by which God is seen. We who have been blessed by God must be witnesses to his goodness. It has been told that a small child was asked who the saints are. Looking up at the stained glass windows, he said, "They are the people the light shines through." May all of us pilgrim saints allow God's light to shine through us each day.

• • • • • • ON THE WAY TO MASS

Who is your role model? Why is this person a good role model?

ON THE WAY HOME FROM MASS • • • • • •

What does it mean to be a light for the world?

Living the Word

This week we will observe Valentine's Day. It is traditionally a day when we let people know that we love them. Besides preparing Valentine cards for classmates, friends, and family, ask your children to think about who else might need to know they are loved. Your children might draw a picture or write a short letter to send to them. Such thoughtfulness is sure to brighten the recipients' day.

February 16, 2020

Sixth Sunday in Ordinary Time

Hearing the Word

Matthew 5:21–22a, 27–28, 33–34a, 37

In the name of the Father, and of the Son, and of the Holy Spirit.

[Jesus said to his disciples:] "You have heard that it was said to your ancestors, / *You shall not kill; and whoever kills will be liable to judgment.* / But I say to you, whoever is angry with his brother will be liable to judgment.

"You have heard that it was said, / *You shall not commit adultery.* / But I say to you, everyone who looks at a woman with lust has already committed adultery with her in his heart.

"Again, you have heard that it was said to your ancestors, *Do not take a false oath, but make good to the Lord all that you vow.* / But I say to you, do not swear at all. Let your 'Yes' mean 'Yes,' and your 'No' mean 'No.' Anything more is from the evil one."

Reflecting on the Word

As Jewish Christians who had always been faithful to the Law, Matthew's community need a way to understand how Jesus takes this understanding of the Law even further. Following the law is more than just rote obedience: we must take the law to heart. We must not only eliminate violent conduct, but also angry thoughts; not only greedy actions, but also selfish desires; not only dishonest words, but also deceitful plans. When we follow the law in our hearts, we build up relationships: with ourselves, with others, and most importantly, with God. We conform ourselves more and more to Christ. We live a life built on and sustained by love.

......ON THE WAY TO MASS

The *Catechism of the Catholic Church* teaches us about our faith. In what other ways do we learn about God and about Jesus' teachings?

ON THE WAY HOME FROM MASS ......

How did Jesus challenge his disciples to follow the Law? How does he challenge you?

Living the Word

Jesus teaches that we should mean what we say and say what we mean. This week, pay attention to how you use words. How are you honest with one another? with classmates or teammates? with friends? Discuss with your children why truth and honesty are important to good, healthy personal relationships.

Seventh Sunday in Ordinary Time

Hearing the Word
Matthew 5:38–48

In the name of the Father, and of the Son, and of the Holy Spirit.

Jesus said to his disciples, "You have heard that it was said, / *An eye for an eye and a tooth for a tooth.* / But I say to you, offer no resistance to the one who is evil. When someone strikes you on your right cheek, turn the other one to him as well. If anyone wants to go to law with you over your tunic, hand him your cloak as well. Should anyone press you into service for one mile, go with him for two miles. Give to the one who asks of you, and do not turn your back on one who wants to borrow.

"You have heard that it was said, / *You shall love your neighbor and hate your enemy.* / But I say to you, love your enemies, and pray for those who persecute you, that you may be children of your heavenly Father, for he makes his sun rise on the bad and the good, and causes rain to fall on the just and the unjust. For if you love those who love you, what recompense will you have? Do not the tax collectors do the same? And if you greet your brothers only, what is unusual about that? Do not the pagans do the same? So be perfect, just as your heavenly Father is perfect."

Reflecting on the Word

The automatic reaction to injury is to lash out with angry words or actions. Christ turns this reaction on its head. Being his follower is not easy. Reaching the perfection that Jesus speaks of will require us asking God for help sometimes.

......ON THE WAY TO MASS

What does it mean to love your enemy? Do you think that will be easy or hard to do?

ON THE WAY HOME FROM MASS ......

How did you understand Jesus' words? How would you follow Jesus' words in today's Gospel?

Living the Word

Pray for those who have hurt you this week. Ask each family member to write down the names of one or more people who have hurt them (it could be recently or a long time ago), and put the slips of paper in a basket on your prayer table. Pray for those people every night (if you feel comfortable, choose a few slips each night and read the names aloud). At the end of the week, discuss how it felt to pray for those who have injured you. Why does Jesus ask us to love our enemies? How is that a step toward peace?

March 1, 2020

First Sunday of Lent

Hearing the Word

Matthew 4:1–4

In the name of the Father, and of the Son, and of the Holy Spirit.

At that time Jesus was led by the Spirit into the desert
to be tempted by the devil. He fasted for forty days and
forty nights, and afterwards he was hungry. The tempter
approached and said to him, "If you are the Son of God,
command that these stones become loaves of bread."
He said in reply, "It is written: / *One does not live by bread
alone, / but on every word that comes forth / from the
mouth of God.*"

Reflecting on the Word

At the beginning of his public ministry, Jesus was tempted by the devil in several ways. The first was the simplest: he was hungry, and was tempted with food. Obviously, bread is not evil in and of itself. Satan tempted Jesus not just to fulfill his hunger, but also to abandon faith in God, in God's care for him, God's sustenance, and God's love. In the face of this temptation, Jesus made a statement of faith instead—that God was all the nourishment he needed. Jesus' rejection of Satan's temptations shows that he will not put God to the test. Establishing himself on the word and authority of Scripture, Jesus rebukes the devil, confident in God's protection and faithfulness.

......ON THE WAY TO MASS

Do you trust in God?

ON THE WAY HOME FROM MASS ......

Have you ever been tempted to sin? What happened?

Living the Word

During Lent, we are asked to give alms, fast, and pray. This Lent, consider what keeps you from trusting in God to sustain you. Maybe it is pride, or love of esteem, or valuing possessions too much. What are some commitments you can make to show faith in God? What do you need to fast from? Where should you put your financial and material bounty? How can you grow closer to God through prayer? The goal of these commitments is not "self-help" but growth in faith. How can you grow closer to God in these forty days?

March 8, 2020

Second Sunday of Lent

Hearing the Word
Matthew 17:1–5

In the name of the Father, and of the Son, and of the Holy Spirit.

Jesus took Peter, James, and John his brother, and led them up a high mountain by themselves. And he was transfigured before them; his face shone like the sun and his clothes became white as light. And behold, Moses and Elijah appeared to them, conversing with him. Then Peter said to Jesus in reply, "Lord, it is good that we are here. If you wish, I will make three tents here, one for you, one for Moses, and one for Elijah." While he was still speaking, behold, a bright cloud cast a shadow over them, then from the cloud came a voice that said, "This is my beloved Son, with whom I am well pleased; listen to him."

Reflecting on the Word

It is good that we are here. We wish that some moments in life would last forever: a fun vacation or great day with friends or even just a cozy night at home. Peter proposed putting up tents and staying on the mountain forever. But the moment could not last, as Jesus and his disciples came down from the mountain and traveled on to Jerusalem, to betrayal, suffering, and death. But the sheer joy of the Transfiguration gave them (and us!) a ray of hope, the strength to persevere in the face of human sorrow and suffering.

• • • • • • ON THE WAY TO MASS

Have you ever wished that a moment would last forever? Why?

ON THE WAY HOME FROM MASS • • • • • •

What did the Transfiguration reveal about Jesus? How did it change the disciples who were there?

Living the Word

Music can elicit strong emotions and memories. Listen to "The Transfiguration" by Sufjan Stevens. (Find it online.) After you listen once, ask each member of the family to offer one reaction to the song. How did it tell the story of the Transfiguration? What do the lyrics say about Jesus? about the disciples? about God? How do rhythm, melody, and harmony each help paint the picture of the Transfiguration in your mind?

Third Sunday of Lent

Hearing the Word

John 4:6–10

In the name of the Father, and of the Son, and of the Holy Spirit.

Jesus, tired about his journey, sat down there at the well. It was about noon.

A woman of Samaria came to draw water. Jesus said to her, "Give me a drink." His disciples had gone into the town to buy food. The Samaritan woman said to him, "How can you, a Jew, ask me, a Samaritan woman, for a drink?"—For Jews use nothing in common with Samaritans.—Jesus answered and said to her, "If you knew the gift of God and who is saying to you, 'Give me a drink,' you would have asked him and he would have given you living water."

Reflecting on the Word

In today's Gospel, Jesus approaches the Samaritan woman first. This is a story of conversion: God holds out a hand of friendship that we might learn to seek his grace. Our reward for reaching out in return is tremendous: living water, water to wash away sin and death, to share in the divine life. God relentlessly pursues his people, at every time and every place. How has God pursued a relationship with you? How do you respond to his call?

......ON THE WAY TO MASS

Explore what it means to thirst physically. How do you feel when you're thirsty?

ON THE WAY HOME FROM MASS ......

The notion of thirst in today's Gospel moves from the physical to the spiritual. We hear that Jesus' offer of living water will quench a spiritual thirst. What is the living water?

Living the Word

This week, learn more about the efforts of Catholic Relief Services (CRS.org) to provide clean water to people around the world. Discuss how your family accesses clean water for drinking, cooking, and cleaning, and contrast it with the situations of others living in poverty or war-torn areas. Consider doing one of the family activities at http://education.crs.org /resources/families. Pray that all people worldwide might have access to clean water.

March 22, 2020

Fourth Sunday of Lent

Hearing the Word

John 9:1–3, 6–7

In the name of the Father, and of the Son, and of the Holy Spirit.

As Jesus passed by he saw a man blind from birth. His disciples asked him, "Rabbi, who sinned, this man or his parents, that he was born blind?" Jesus answered, "Neither he nor his parents sinned; it is so that the works of God might be made visible through him." When he had said this, he spat on the ground and made clay with the saliva, and smeared the clay on his eyes, and said to him, "Go wash in the Pool of Siloam"—which means Sent—. So he went and washed, and came back able to see.

Reflecting on the Word

In today's Gospel, we are invited to focus on the physical and spiritual aspects of sight and light. Jesus responds to the prevalent belief of his time that misfortune and disability were the result of sin. He responds by giving the question a different twist—that through this man's disability, God's power will be made known.

God makes himself visible through our lives, through the good or happy occurrences. But sometimes, as with the man born blind, we come to know God through the challenges we face. God works in us, even in dark times, shining a light of hope and faith and offering healing for body, heart, or soul. God not only works in us, but also walks with us through all the good and the bad.

······ ON THE WAY TO MASS

What might it be like not to physically see?

ON THE WAY HOME FROM MASS ······

What might it be like not to recognize God's presence in our lives? How might our lives be different in each of these scenarios?

Living the Word

Are there people in your community whom you fail to notice? Perhaps it is the elderly, the sick or homebound of your parish, the homeless, or those living in precarious financial situations. Do you see Christ in them? Choose a person or group that you can pray for this week, and commit to being present to them, to see and love them, and to care for them as tenderly as you would care for Christ.

March 29, 2020

FIFTH SUNDAY OF LENT

Hearing the Word

John 11:17–23

In the name of the Father, and of the Son, and of the Holy Spirit.

When Jesus arrived, he found that Lazarus had already been in the tomb for four days. Now Bethany was near Jerusalem, only about two miles away. And many of the Jews had come to Martha and Mary to comfort them about their brother. When Martha heard that Jesus was coming, she went to meet him; but Mary sat at home. Martha said to Jesus, "Lord, if you had been here, my brother would not have died. But even now I know that whatever you ask of God, God will give you." Jesus said to her, "Your brother will rise."

Reflecting on the Word

The context for today's Gospel reading is the Jewish leaders' growing hostility toward Jesus. Jesus has been in Jerusalem, and the people have been pressing him to pronounce plainly that he is the Messiah. Jesus tells them to decide for themselves by looking to his works, which testify to his coming from God.

As you listen to this story, another of Jesus' miracles, we are reminded that death is not an end to life; rather, it leads to life anew. We recognize that it is still painful when death separates us from our loved one. But we also remember the promise that, like Lazarus, we too will one day rise.

......ON THE WAY TO MASS

Have you ever had to comfort someone who experienced the death of a loved one? Have you ever been the one who was comforted?

ON THE WAY HOME FROM MASS ......

How did Martha express faith in Jesus? How can you trust Jesus in the same way?

Living the Word

If possible, go with your children to a loved one's gravesite. Share memories. Read John 11:17–44 aloud. Discuss how Mary and Martha and their friends must have felt when Lazarus died. How do you think they reacted when he walked out of the tomb? How would you react if you were there? What does this story tell us about God? Pray for all of the dead, that they might rise to new life like Lazarus did.

April 5, 2020

Palm Sunday of the Passion of the Lord

Hearing the Word

Matthew 21:1–11

In the name of the Father, and of the Son, and of the Holy Spirit.

When Jesus and the disciples drew near Jerusalem and
came to Bethphage on the Mount of Olives, Jesus sent two
disciples, saying to them, "Go into the village opposite you,
and immediately you will find an ass tethered, and a colt
with her. Untie them and bring them here to me. And if
anyone should say anything to you, reply, 'The master
has need of them.' Then he will send them at once." This
happened so that what had been spoken through the
prophet might be fulfilled: / *Say to daughter Zion, / "Behold,
your king comes to you, / meek and riding on an ass, / and
on a colt, the foal of a beast of burden." /* The disciples went
and did as Jesus had ordered them. They brought the ass
and the colt and laid their cloaks over them, and he sat
upon them. The very large crowd spread their cloaks on
the road, while others cut branches from the trees and
strewed them on the road. The crowds preceding him and
those following kept crying out and saying: / "Hosanna
to the Son of David; / blessed is he who comes in the name
of the Lord; / hosanna in the highest." / And when he
entered Jerusalem the whole city was shaken and asked,
"Who is this?" And the crowds replied, "This is Jesus the
prophet, from Nazareth in Galilee."

Reflecting on the Word

The Palm Sunday liturgy begins in triumph and ends in darkness. The same crowds that joyfully welcome Jesus as he enters Jerusalem are to turn against him just a few days later. They will jeer at him and condemn him. They ignore the Truth they have seen with their own eyes. How many times have we ignored the Truth that has been revealed to us? turned a blind eye to the presence of God in our lives? forsaken truth and goodness in the face of societal pressure?

......ON THE WAY TO MASS

Alert your family that we begin Holy Week today. Palm Sunday is a day of high emotions: happiness and heartbreak.

ON THE WAY HOME FROM MASS ......

We heard today that Jesus obeyed his Father's will, even when he was scared and he faced certain death. How do you understand God's will for you?

Living the Word

We began Lent by receiving ashes, which were burned from last year's palm branches. Today we begin Holy Week and receive new blessed palms. Look for tutorials online to fashion the palms into crosses. You might have your children process through the house singing "All Glory Laud and Honor" or another appropriate hymn. Place a palm cross over the doors or behind a crucifix.

April 12, 2020

Easter Sunday of the Resurrection of the Lord

Hearing the Word

John 20:1–8

In the name of the Father, and of the Son, and of the Holy Spirit.

On the first day of the week, Mary of Magdala came to the tomb early in the morning, while it was still dark, and saw the stone removed from the tomb. So she ran and went to Simon Peter and to the other disciple whom Jesus loved, and told them, "They have taken the Lord from the tomb, and we don't know where they put him." So Peter and the other disciple went out and came to the tomb. They both ran, but the other disciple ran faster than Peter and arrived at the tomb first; he bent down and saw the burial cloths there, but did not go in. When Simon Peter arrived after him, he went into the tomb and saw the burial cloths there, and the cloth that had covered his head, not with the burial cloths but rolled up in a separate place. Then the other disciple also went in, the one who had arrived at the tomb first, and he saw and believed.

Reflecting on the Word

The story begins in darkness, which is symbolic as the realization of the empty tomb dawns on Mary of Magdala. It is probably light by the time she returns to the tomb accompanied by the two disciples. Simon Peter enters the empty tomb, but the first disciple ahead of him is the one who believes upon seeing the burial cloths. There is indeed a glimpse of new life in this account, but even richer is the truth that the stone is rolled back and that Christ's Resurrection signifies triumph over death. The details in John's account invite us to reflect upon a most amazing gift: faith in Christ and his Resurrection.

•••••• ON THE WAY TO MASS

Have your family pay close attention to the changes in the church today. How is the joy of Easter expressed in the colors they see? in the music they hear? in the scents they smell?

ON THE WAY HOME FROM MASS ••••••

Ask your children to recall what they noticed at Mass. How do they know the Mass was more joyfully celebrated today?

Living the Word

Christ is risen, Alleluia! We are celebrating the greatest mystery of our faith: that death has been vanquished by the power of God's love. Celebrate Easter lavishly, and continue celebrating the whole week! Plan special outings with friends and family. Sing Alleluia at prayer time. Fill your house with flowers (a sign of new life). Bring treats and flowers to those who are homebound, far from family, or feeling lonely.

April 19, 2020

Second Sunday of Easter / Sunday of Divine Mercy

Hearing the Word

John 20:19–29

In the name of the Father, and of the Son, and of the Holy Spirit.

On the evening of that first day of the week, when the doors were locked, where the disciples were, . . . Jesus came and stood in their midst and said to them, "Peace be with you." When he had said this, he showed them his hands and his side. The disciples rejoiced when they saw the Lord. Jesus said to them again, "Peace be with you. As the Father has sent me, so I send you." And when he had said this, he breathed on them and said to them, "Receive the Holy Spirit. Whose sins you forgive are forgiven them, and whose sins you retain are retained."

Thomas, called Didymus, one of the Twelve, was not with them when Jesus came. So the other disciples said to him, "We have seen the Lord." But he said to them, "Unless I see the mark of the nails in his hands and put my finger into the nailmarks and put my hand into his side, I will not believe."

Now a week later . . . Jesus came . . . and said, "Peace be with you." Then he said to Thomas, "Put your finger here and see my hands, and bring your hand and put it into my side, and do not be unbelieving, but believe." Thomas answered and said to him, "My Lord and my God!" Jesus said to him, "Have you come to believe because you have seen me? Blessed are those who have not seen and have believed."

Reflecting on the Word

Faith would be so much easier if only we had tangible confirmation. We will likely not put our fingers through the holes in Christ's hands. But "faith is the realization of what is hoped for and evidence of things not seen" (Hebrews 11:1). When Thomas at last meets the Lord, he knows him immediately and cries out in joy and faith. We will meet Jesus in many surprising ways through life. May we too have the faith to exclaim, "My Lord and my God!"

••••••ON THE WAY TO MASS

Do you find it hard to have faith in God? What is most challenging for you?

ON THE WAY HOME FROM MASS ••••••

Where have you met Jesus? How has your encounter with Jesus led to greater faith?

Living the Word

Today is also known as Divine Mercy Sunday. Learn about the life of St. Faustina and her mission to make God's mercy known the world. Print or buy the image of the Divine Mercy (or print coloring sheets for your children) and place it on your prayer table. Together, pray the Divine Mercy chaplet. Information about Divine Mercy Sunday, St. Faustina, and the chaplet can be found at http://www.usccb.org/about /pro-life-activities/prayers/divine-mercy-sunday.cfm.

April 26, 2020

Third Sunday of Easter

Hearing the Word

Luke 24:13–15, 30–32

In the name of the Father, and of the Son, and of the Holy Spirit.

That very day, the first day of the week, two of Jesus' disciples were going to a village seven miles from Jerusalem called Emmaus, and they were conversing about all the things that had occurred. And it happened that while they were conversing and debating, Jesus himself drew near and walked with them. And it happened that, while he was with them at table, he took bread, said the blessing, broke it, and gave it to them. With that their eyes were opened and they recognized him, but he vanished from their sight. Then they said to each other, "Were not our hearts burning within us while he spoke to us on the way and opened the Scriptures to us?"

Reflecting on the Word

The two disciples poured out their fear and sadness to the stranger they met on the road. They did not recognize him until his breaking of the bread. In this Gospel, we learn that the Risen Christ is not always easily recognized. Sometimes we only recognize Jesus in hindsight. But, whether we know him or not, Jesus draws near to all of us on the journey of life. He is there to remind us of the Truth, to reassure us in the dark times, to light our way.

......ON THE WAY TO MASS

Have you ever met someone new and, right away, connected with that person? Why do we feel chemistry with certain people?

Ask your family to pay special attention to when the priest breaks the bread during the Liturgy of the Eucharist.

ON THE WAY HOME FROM MASS ......

What connection do you see between today's Gospel and the liturgy? In the Eucharist, we share in the breaking of the bread and find Christ in our midst. Just as the disciples returned to Jerusalem to recount their experience to the other disciples, we too are sent from our Eucharistic gathering to share our experience with others.

Living the Word

Why did the disciples say their hearts were burning within? Discuss how the disciples might have felt before being joined by Jesus, and then when they traveled with him. Imagine how they reacted when Jesus was revealed to them. Talk about what it means for your heart to be burning within you.

May 3, 2020

Fourth Sunday of Easter

Hearing the Word

John 10:1–10

In the name of the Father, and of the Son, and of the Holy Spirit.

Jesus said, "Amen, amen, I say to you, whoever does not enter a sheepfold through the gate but climbs over elsewhere is a thief and a robber. But whoever enters through the gate is the shepherd of the sheep. The gatekeeper opens it for him, and the sheep hear his voice, as the shepherd calls his own sheep by name and leads them out. When he has driven out all his own, he walks ahead of them, and the sheep follow him, because they recognize his voice. But they will not follow a stranger; they will run away from him, because they do not recognize the voice of strangers." Although Jesus used this figure of speech, the Pharisees did not realize what he was trying to tell them.

So Jesus said again, "Amen, amen, I say to you, I am the gate for the sheep. All who came before me are thieves and robbers, but the sheep did not listen to them. I am the gate. Whoever enters through me will be saved, and will come in and go out and find pasture. A thief comes only to steal and slaughter and destroy; I came so that they might have life and have it more abundantly."

Reflecting on the Word

Sheep will distinguish the voice of their shepherd from all other voices. They trust that their shepherd will lead them well and in safety. Jesus is the Good Shepherd, and we are his sheep. He loves us and calls us each by name. If we follow him, he will guide us to eternal happiness. It is up to us to know and heed his voice amid the clamor of other voices that try to lead us astray. What can only separate us from God is our own free choice to turn away.

......ON THE WAY TO MASS

What do you know about sheep and shepherds? Listen to today's Gospel and think about why Jesus would use the idea of shepherds and sheep to teach about God's Kingdom.

ON THE WAY HOME FROM MASS ......

Explain to your children that the Fourth Sunday of Easter is known as Good Shepherd Sunday. Each year we hear a different reading about Jesus comparing himself to a shepherd leading his sheep. Who are today's "good shepherds" who lead us in faithfulness? (Suggested answers: pope, pastors, Christian leaders.)

Living the Word

How does a shepherd care for his sheep? How does God care for his people? Ask each family member to explain how God has cared for him or her. How does it make you feel to know that God loves you and calls you by name? Close by listening to or singing a musical arrangement of Psalm 23. Ask your children how they feel when they listen to the words of the psalm (comfort, love, being protected).

May 10, 2020

Fifth Sunday of Easter

Hearing the Word

John 14:1–10a

In the name of the Father, and of the Son, and of the Holy Spirit.

Jesus said to his disciples, "Do not let your hearts be troubled. You have faith in God; have faith also in me. In my Father's house there are many dwelling places. If there were not, would I have told you that I am going to prepare a place for you? And if I go and prepare a place for you, I will come back again and take you to myself, so that where I am you also may be. Where I am going you know the way." Thomas said to him, "Master, we do not know where you are going; how can we know the way?" Jesus said to him, "I am the way and the truth and the life. No one comes to the Father except through me. If you know me, then you will also know my Father. From now on you do know him and have seen him." Philip said to him, "Master, show us the Father, and that will be enough for us." Jesus said to him, "Have I been with you for so long a time and you still do not know me, Philip? Whoever has seen me has seen the Father. How can you say, 'Show us the Father'? Do you not believe that I am in the Father and the Father is in me?"

Reflecting on the Word

Do not let your hearts be troubled. These are some of the last words Jesus offers to his disciples. Do not let your hearts be troubled when faced with despair, suffering, or loss. Do not allow the world to break you. This seems easier said than done, especially when we are confronted by the deep pain the world can bring. Jesus says he is the way, the truth, and the life. He is the way of hope, healing, and light in the darkest night. He is the way to eternal joy.

......ON THE WAY TO MASS

Have you ever felt sad or confused or lonely? Did you ever lose your way and felt scared? When has your heart been troubled?

ON THE WAY HOME FROM MASS ......

Discuss with your family the following: Jesus doesn't want us to feel troubled. He wants us to believe in him and to trust him. Jesus has shown us the way to live good lives as sons and daughters of God. He has taught us the truth about God and his great love, and through him, we will have everlasting life with God in heaven.

Living the Word

Have your children cut out a dozen little hearts from construction paper. Ask them first to think about how Jesus doesn't want our hearts to be troubled. On each little heart, have them write one way they can show God's love to one another. Remind them to write their names on the hearts.

Sixth Sunday of Easter

Hearing the Word

John 14:15–21

In the name of the Father, and of the Son, and of the Holy Spirit.

Jesus said to his disciples, "If you love me, you will keep my commandments. And I will ask the Father, and he will give you another Advocate to be with you always, the Spirit of truth, whom the world cannot accept, because it neither sees nor knows him. But you know him, because he remains with you, and will be in you. I will not leave you orphans; I will come to you. In a little while the world will no longer see me, but you will see me, because I live and you will live. On that day you will realize that I am in my Father and you are in me and I in you. Whoever has my commandments and observes them is the one who loves me. And whoever loves me will be loved by my Father, and I will love him and reveal myself to him."

Reflecting on the Word

Jesus proposes something revolutionary to the disciples: that God will come and inhabit them, that their own hearts will become temples of the Holy Spirit. If we surrender ourselves to God, he will come and live in us and we in him. We will be as close as a heartbeat. God offers us a relationship of love, the love that truly desires the good of the other. And his love bears fruit as it teaches us to see with God's eyes, to follow not the ways of the world but the Way of Love.

•••••• ON THE WAY TO MASS

What words or actions express love? How do you know you are loved?

ON THE WAY HOME FROM MASS ••••••

How do we show our love to one another at home? How can we be better about showing one another our love—to one another, to those outside our family, and to God?

Living the Word

"'You shall love the Lord your God with all your heart, with all your soul, with all your mind, and with all your strength.' The second [commandment] is this: 'You shall love your neighbor as yourself.' There is no other commandment greater than these" (Mark 12:30–31). Jesus' exhortation to share God's love is challenging in its simplicity. Think of some ways you can live these two commandments, both individually and as a family.

May 21, 2020

Solemnity of the Ascension of the Lord

Hearing the Word

Matthew 28:16–20

In the name of the Father, and of the Son, and of the Holy Spirit.

The eleven disciples went to Galilee, to the mountain to which Jesus had ordered them. When they saw him, they worshiped, but they doubted. Then Jesus approached and said to them, "All power in heaven and on earth has been given to me. Go, therefore, and make disciples of all nations, baptizing them in the name of the Father, and of the Son, and of the Holy Spirit, teaching them to observe all that I have commanded you. And behold, I am with you always, until the end of the age."

Reflecting on the Word

In their last earthly encounter with Jesus, we hear that the disciples worshipped, but they doubted. This seems to be a paradox. How could the disciples worship Jesus Christ and at the same time doubt the truth of his identity? But Jesus is not concerned with their doubt, just as he was not concerned with their betrayal in Jerusalem. He exhorts them to make disciples of all nations. Even when we, like the disciples, doubt and deny and are imperfect, we are still called to be missionaries of his Good News.

•••••• ON THE WAY TO MASS

Have you ever felt insecure and unready, yet excited and hopeful about something new?

ON THE WAY HOME FROM MASS ••••••

Jesus left his followers in the care of the Holy Spirit. How do we feel the presence of the Spirit today?

Living the Word

Images are important reminders of people we love. That is why we carry photos in wallets and phones, or place them on our dressers, desks, or living room walls. Similarly, the presence of religious art in the home can be a way of remembering our relationship to God. Look for images or statues that resonate with your family and display them in your prayer space or in your children's rooms.

May 24, 2020

Seventh Sunday of Easter

Hearing the Word

John 17:1–11a

In the name of the Father, and of the Son, and of the Holy Spirit.

Jesus raised his eyes to heaven and said, "Father, the hour has come. Give glory to your son, so that your son may glorify you, just as you gave him authority over all people, so that your son may give eternal life to all you gave him. Now this is eternal life, that they should know you, the only true God, and the one whom you sent, Jesus Christ. I glorified you on earth by accomplishing the work that you gave me to do. Now glorify me, Father, with you, with the glory that I had with you before the world began.

"I revealed your name to those whom you gave me out of the world. They belonged to you, and you gave them to me, and they have kept your word. Now they know that everything you gave me is from you, because the words you gave to me I have given to them, and they accepted them and truly understood that I came from you, and they have believed that you sent me. I pray for them. I do not pray for the world but for the ones you have given me, because they are yours, and everything of mine is yours and everything of yours is mine, and I have been glorified in them. And now I will no longer be in the world, but they are in the world, while I am coming to you."

Reflecting on the Word

Today's Gospel may sound very abstract and difficult to relate to. Perhaps a key phrase is at the end of this excerpt, when Jesus speaks of the glory he had with the Father "before the world began." This leads us into the mystery of the Most Holy Trinity, which we will celebrate in a few weeks. For now, it is enough to meditate on the fact that Jesus Christ—who walked the earth as a human being, as one of us—is one with God, who is eternal, without beginning or end.

⋯⋯ ON THE WAY TO MASS

Instruct your children to listen carefully to the words, especially the beginning of the Creed, which we say after the Homily. (You may wish to refer to the Apostles' Creed on page 117.)

ON THE WAY HOME FROM MASS ⋯⋯

Explain what the Creed is and why we profess our faith every Sunday. What is the connection between today's Gospel and the Creed?

Living the Word

Read the Apostles' Creed together. Talk about how it contains the essential beliefs of our Catholic faith.

Pentecost Sunday

Hearing the Word

John 20:19–23

In the name of the Father, and of the Son, and of the Holy Spirit.

On the evening of that first day of the week, when the doors were locked, where the disciples were, for fear of the Jews, Jesus came and stood in their midst and said to them, "Peace be with you." When he had said this, he showed them his hands and his side. The disciples rejoiced when they saw the Lord. Jesus said to them again, "Peace be with you. As the Father has sent me, so I send you." And when he had said this, he breathed on them and said to them, "Receive the Holy Spirit. Whose sins you forgive are forgiven them, and whose sins you retain are retained."

Reflecting on the Word

It is now fifty days since Easter Sunday, and we complete our celebration of Easter with Pentecost (*pentecoste* means "fiftieth"). Notice that twice Jesus says, "Peace be with you" to the frightened disciples. In the same encounter, he gives them the power to forgive sins. Sin is a rupture in our relationship with God, with others, and even with ourselves. It is difficult to experience peace when we are out of good or right relationship.

•••••• ON THE WAY TO MASS

Today is another opportunity to reflect on the connection between the Gospel and the liturgy. Ask your children to notice what Jesus says twice to the disciples. When will they say the same words in the Mass?

ON THE WAY HOME FROM MASS ••••••

What is having peace like? What is it like to give and to receive peace?

Living the Word

On the feast of Pentecost, we celebrate the coming of the Holy Spirit and institution of the Church. Punctuate your family's feast with touches of the color red: red roses, red tablecloth, red cake (with seven candles to signify the seven gifts of the Holy Spirit). Have your children make simple paper doves to decorate your prayer space. Pray the sequence for Pentecost (*Veni, Sancte Spiritus*) in English or Latin (or both!).

June 7, 2020

Solemnity of the Most Holy Trinity

Hearing the Word

John 3:16–18

In the name of the Father, and of the Son, and of the Holy Spirit.

God so loved the world that he gave his only Son, so that everyone who believes in him might not perish but might have eternal life. For God did not send his Son into the world to condemn the world, but that the world might be saved through him. Whoever believes in him will not be condemned, but whoever does not believe has already been condemned, because he has not believed in the name of the only Son of God.

Reflecting on the Word

The *Catechism of the Catholic Church* calls the doctrine of the Trinity "the central mystery of the Christian faith." The Trinity is the mystery of God's very identity—God is Love. Through the revelation of the Trinity, we learn that the inner life of God is communion. The love they share is so great, it has been overflowed out into creation and into each of us. So let us also contemplate the mystery of ourselves, that we have been made, formed, and destined for love.

• • • • • • ON THE WAY TO MASS

Which Person of the Holy Trinity do you relate to best: God the Father, Jesus Christ (God's Son), or the Holy Spirit?

ON THE WAY HOME FROM MASS • • • • • •

What does it mean to say that God is Love? What does that mean for your life?

Living the Word

Find a selection of depictions of the Holy Trinity in fine art throughout the ages (icons, painting, sculpture) and share them with your family. Discuss what each depiction tells us about the Trinity. For prayer this day, begin by crossing yourselves (using holy water if you have it) and praying that we might live in God's love. Close your family prayer by praying or listening to the *Te Deum*, the beautiful chant of praise and thanksgiving to the Triune God.

Solemnity of the Most Holy Body and Blood of Christ

Hearing the Word

John 6:51–58

In the name of the Father, and of the Son, and of the Holy Spirit.

Jesus said to the Jewish crowds: "I am the living bread that came down from heaven; whoever eats this bread will live forever; and the bread that I will give is my flesh for the life of the world."

The Jews quarreled among themselves, saying, "How can this man give us his flesh to eat?" Jesus said to them, "Amen, amen, I say to you, unless you eat the flesh of the Son of Man and drink his blood, you do not have life within you. Whoever eats my flesh and drinks my blood has eternal life, and I will raise him on the last day. For my flesh is true food, and my blood is true drink. Whoever eats my flesh and drinks my blood remains in me and I in him. Just as the living Father sent me and I have life because of the Father, so also the one who feeds on me will have life because of me. This is the bread that came down from heaven. Unlike your ancestors who ate and still died, whoever eats this bread will live forever."

Reflecting on the Word

The mystery of the Eucharist is the mystery of our union with Jesus Christ. Each time we partake of the Body and Blood of Christ, we behold the living God, and we allow Christ to fill and transform every corner of our lives. Jesus himself becomes our nourishment, our strength for a life of discipleship. And in each celebration, we are given new life—the life of Christ. We are uniquely and completely transformed and reformed into Christ.

......ON THE WAY TO MASS

We need to eat nourishing food every day to grow, to be strong, and to be healthy. What do we have to do to have strong and healthy spiritual lives?

ON THE WAY HOME FROM MASS ......

For older children: What does it mean to you to receive Holy Communion?

For younger children: What about First Communion are you looking forward to?

Living the Word

Eucharistic processions and adoration are a tradition on this solemnity, and are a great way to revere the mystery of the Eucharist. Participate in one if you can. Or spend time as a family in Eucharistic adoration this day. Give thanks for the great gift of Christ's Body and Blood. Close the day's celebration by singing or saying St. Thomas Aquinas' famous Eucharistic hymn *Pange Lingua Gloriosi*.

June 21, 2020

Twelfth Sunday in Ordinary Time

Hearing the Word

Matthew 10:26–33

In the name of the Father, and of the Son, and of the Holy Spirit.

Jesus said to the Twelve: "Fear no one. Nothing is concealed that will not be revealed, nor secret that will not be known. What I say to you in the darkness, speak in the light; what you hear whispered, proclaim on the housetops. And do not be afraid of those who kill the body but cannot kill the soul; rather, be afraid of the one who can destroy both soul and body in Gehenna. Are not two sparrows sold for a small coin? Yet not one of them falls to the ground without your Father's knowledge. Even all the hairs of your head are counted. So do not be afraid; you are worth more than many sparrows. Everyone who acknowledges me before others I will acknowledge before my heavenly Father. But whoever denies me before others, I will deny before my heavenly Father."

Reflecting on the Word

Emphasizing God's wisdom, Jesus instructs his Apostles on how to live openly in God's love. If God cares for the tiny sparrows, he would care for us even more. No matter is too small for God. We only have to trust in him.

● ● ● ● ● ● ON THE WAY TO MASS

How do you know God is watching over you?

ON THE WAY HOME FROM MASS ● ● ● ● ● ●

How has God been with you in times of fear, grief, or pain? What about the happy, joyful times?

Living the Word

We all need reassurance about God's love and care. It is important to demonstrate your belief that your family is precious and cared for by God in your prayer and your actions. If there are particular problems or anxieties that you are struggling with, bring them to God in prayer with your family. If there is something one of your children is struggling with or afraid of, encourage him or her to ask God for his protection and help. Trust in God's care.

June 28, 2020

Thirteenth Sunday in Ordinary Time

Hearing the Word

Matthew 10:37–42

In the name of the Father, and of the Son, and of the Holy Spirit.

Jesus said to his apostles: "Whoever loves father or mother more than me is not worthy of me, and whoever loves son or daughter more than me is not worthy of me; and whoever does not take up his cross and follow after me is not worthy of me. Whoever finds his life will lose it, and whoever loses his life for my sake will find it.

"Whoever receives you receives me, and whoever receives me receives the one who sent me. Whoever receives a prophet because he is a prophet will receive a prophet's reward, and whoever receives a righteous man because he is righteous will receive a righteous man's reward. And whoever gives only a cup of cold water to one of these little ones to drink because he is a disciple—amen, I say to you, he will surely not lose his reward."

Reflecting on the Word

Jesus is very clear. We must love God more than we love our families, more than we love our own lives. This means putting God before all else: family obligations, work, leisure. It means focusing on God at all times instead of confining our love for God to convenient moments. Paradoxically, when we love God best, our capacity for love expands. We love everyone better; we lavish our family, friends, coworkers, and neighbors with God's love—a limitless, patient, unconditional love.

•••••• ON THE WAY TO MASS

What does love mean to you?

ON THE WAY HOME FROM MASS ••••••

What does it mean for you to love God more than your family or yourself? How do you show that love? How has God taught you how to love others?

Living the Word

God sees all of us differently than we see ourselves. Ask your children to draw a picture of how they think God sees them. Next, discuss what it means to have "God's eyes" when we look at others. How would God show love for your best friends? for the bully at school? for the homeless person on the street? How does seeing with God's eyes change your view of these people?

FOURTEENTH SUNDAY IN ORDINARY TIME

Hearing the Word

Matthew 11:25–30

In the name of the Father, and of the Son, and of the Holy Spirit.

At that time Jesus exclaimed: "I give praise to you, Father, Lord of heaven and earth, for although you have hidden these things from the wise and the learned you have revealed them to little ones. Yes, Father, such has been your gracious will. All things have been handed over to me by my Father. No one knows the Son except the Father, and no one knows the Father except the Son and anyone to whom the Son wishes to reveal him.

"Come to me, all you who labor and are burdened, and I will give you rest. Take my yoke upon you and learn from me, for I am meek and humble of heart; and you will find rest for yourselves. For my yoke is easy, and my burden light."

Reflecting on the Word

All of us feel weighed down sometimes because of worry, fear, anxiety, despair. When we hang on to these burdens, they grow heavier and heavier until it is difficult to move at all. Jesus urges us to come to him, to share our burdens with him, and allow him to lighten the load we carry. When we open ourselves fully to Jesus, asking him to help us bear even our deepest darkness and shame, he will give us rest and peace. How can you trust Jesus with your burdens?

•••••• ON THE WAY TO MASS

In today's Gospel, Jesus says, "Come to me, all you who labor and are burdened, and I will give you rest." What are your thoughts on this statement?

ON THE WAY HOME FROM MASS ••••••

What burdens (physical, emotional, or spiritual) do you want to give over to Jesus?

Living the Word

Fill two one-gallon milk jugs (one for every child, if possible), with enough water so that they have some weight but are not too heavy for the child. Ask your children to pick them up, and to tell you whether they feel heavy. Have your children pick up a jug and hold it straight in front of them. Use a timer to see who can hold the jug the longest. Then discuss the following questions: Why did the jugs feel heavier the more time that passed? How does this feeling relate to the Gospel?

July 12, 2020

Fifteenth Sunday in Ordinary Time

Hearing the Word

Matthew 13:1–9

In the name of the Father, and of the Son, and of the Holy Spirit.

On that day, Jesus went out of the house and sat down by the sea. Such large crowds gathered around him that he got into a boat and sat down, and the whole crowd stood along the shore. And he spoke to them at length in parables, saying: "A sower went out to sow. And as he sowed, some seed fell on the path, and birds came and ate it up. Some fell on rocky ground, where it had little soil. It sprang up at once because the soil was not deep, and when the sun rose it was scorched, and it withered for lack of roots. Some seed fell among thorns, and the thorns grew up and choked it. But some seed fell on rich soil, and produced fruit, a hundred or sixty or thirtyfold. Whoever has ears ought to hear."

Reflecting on the Word

God is constantly scattering the seed of his Word in our lives. At different times, we might be the vulnerable path, the inhospitable rocks, the hostile thorns, or the rich soil. Our openness to the Word of God changes as we go through fruitful times and barren times, experience joy and sorrow. God does not force us to hear him. But if we transform our hearts into fertile soil, he will sow his Word in us, and his Word will produce abundant fruit: more grace and goodness than we can possibly imagine.

• • • • • • ON THE WAY TO MASS

How do seeds grow?

ON THE WAY HOME FROM MASS • • • • • •

Ask your children to recall what happened to the various seeds. Can we make our hearts into good soil where God's love will grow? How?

Living the Word

A good way for children to meditate on Scripture, particularly the parables, is to have them draw the story. Prepare some paper and coloring materials. Ask your children to focus on today's Gospel by sitting comfortably and paying attention to what you will read. (Use the passage printed on the previous page.) Then have your children draw the four different places where the seed was thrown, using one page per area. There's no need for in-depth explanation at this moment; let the children simply draw and meditate on the Word.

July 19, 2020

Sixteenth Sunday in Ordinary Time

Hearing the Word

Matthew 13:24–30

In the name of the Father, and of the Son, and of the Holy Spirit.

Jesus proposed another parable to the crowds, saying:
"The kingdom of heaven may be likened to a man who
sowed good seed in his field. While everyone was asleep
his enemy came and sowed weeds all through the wheat,
and then went off. When the crop grew and bore fruit,
the weeds appeared as well. The slaves of the householder
came to him and said, 'Master, did you not sow good seed
in your field? Where have the weeds come from?' He
answered, 'An enemy has done this.' His slaves said to him,
'Do you want us to go and pull them up?' He replied, 'No,
if you pull up the weeds you might uproot the wheat along
with them. Let them grow together until harvest; then
at harvest time I will say to the harvesters, "First collect
the weeds and tie them in bundles for burning; but gather
the wheat into my barn."'"

Reflecting on the Word

We all are surrounded by weeds: our own sins and failures, pain and heartache, the evil actions of others, and disasters of the world. These weeds seem to overrun everything that is good in us and in the world. And even still, Jesus urges us to trust in God, to let him judge the wheat from the weeds. For the wheat can still bear good fruit, even when tangled in the weeds. God, the sower of the seed and the one who nourishes the wheat, is also the just judge who will gather the wheat in due time.

......ON THE WAY TO MASS

Has there ever been a time when someone you know has had his or her good work disrupted by someone or something else? Tell your children about it and ask them to listen carefully to today's Gospel.

ON THE WAY HOME FROM MASS ......

After hearing today's Gospel, ask your children for their impressions, particularly in light of the story you told them prior to Mass.

Living the Word

The world we live in isn't black and white. Sometimes it is hard to know what is right or good to do. So, it is important to pray and to be open to the guidance of the Holy Spirit. Although evil exists in the world and bad things happen, God loves us and forgives our sins when we repent. We must always stay focused on loving God and one another. Give thanks to God for his guidance and unconditional love.

July 26, 2020

Seventeenth Sunday in Ordinary Time

Hearing the Word

Matthew 13:44–52

In the name of the Father, and of the Son, and of the Holy Spirit.

Jesus said to his disciples: "The kingdom of heaven is like a treasure buried in a field, which a person finds and hides again, and out of joy goes and sells all that he has and buys that field. Again, the kingdom of heaven is like a merchant searching for fine pearls. When he finds a pearl of great price, he goes and sells all that he has and buys it. Again, the kingdom of heaven is like a net thrown into the sea, which collects fish of every kind. When it is full they haul it ashore and sit down to put what is good into buckets. What is bad they throw away. Thus it will be at the end of the age. The angels will go out and separate the wicked from the righteous and throw them into the fiery furnace, where there will be wailing and grinding of teeth.

"Do you understand all these things?" They answered, "Yes." And he replied, "Then every scribe who has been instructed in the kingdom of heaven is like the head of a household who brings from his storeroom both the new and the old."

Reflecting on the Word

In these parables, Jesus explains how priceless the Kingdom of Heaven is. Jesus teaches us that God's Kingdom is like these treasures. What would you compare the Kingdom of Heaven to? In order to possess the Kingdom of God, we must be willing to give all that we have, to risk our safety and security in this world for the sake of the next.

• • • • • • ON THE WAY TO MASS

Ask your children what they would be willing to part with to be with God.

ON THE WAY HOME FROM MASS • • • • • •

God is more generous than we can imagine. How has God been generous to you?

Living the Word

Make a treasure box for your prayer table this week. Read the parable of the pearl with your family. Talk about what it meant that the merchant sold all that he had. Does this include his furniture? his clothes? his house? Why was he willing to do that? What is the treasure that we have found in God? Write down responses on slips of paper and put them in the treasure box.

EIGHTEENTH SUNDAY IN ORDINARY TIME

Hearing the Word
Matthew 14:15–20

In the name of the Father, and of the Son, and of the Holy Spirit.

When it was evening, the disciples approached [Jesus] and said, "This is a deserted place and it is already late; dismiss the crowds so that they can go to the villages and buy food for themselves." Jesus said to them, "There is no need for them to go away; give them some food yourselves." But they said to him, "Five loaves and two fish are all we have here." Then he said, "Bring them here to me," and he ordered the crowds to sit down on the grass. Taking the five loaves and the two fish, and looking up to heaven, he said the blessing, broke the loaves, and gave them to the disciples, who in turn gave them to the crowds. They all ate and were satisfied.

Reflecting on the Word

Jesus accepts a modest offering of five loaves and two fish and transforms it, increases it into food for all. So does he transform each of us, when we offer him all that we have. He takes our offering and makes us into his body, food for the life of the world. Today's Gospel is a wonderful story of the abundance that comes from trusting in God and sharing whatever we have. We are reminded that our needs will be met and our hungers satisfied when we live in relationship to God and to one another.

······ ON THE WAY TO MASS

Is it easy to share? When is it harder to share what you have? Why?

ON THE WAY HOME FROM MASS ······

Ask your children to share their thoughts on the Gospel.

Living the Word

Find and read the children's book *Stone Soup* by Ann McGovern. Relate the story to today's Gospel. How might the disciples have felt when Jesus told them to give food to the crowd themselves? What might they have been thinking when they were able to feed everyone in the crowd? How does Jesus transform each of us? How do you feed others?

Nineteenth Sunday in Ordinary Time

Hearing the Word

Matthew 14:26–31

In the name of the Father, and of the Son, and of the Holy Spirit.

When the disciples saw [Jesus] walking on the sea they were terrified. "It is a ghost," they said, and they cried out in fear. At once Jesus spoke to them, "Take courage, it is I; do not be afraid." Peter said to him in reply, "Lord, if it is you, command me to come to you on the water." He said, "Come." Peter got out of the boat and began to walk on the water toward Jesus. But when he saw how strong the wind was he became frightened; and, beginning to sink, he cried out, "Lord, save me!" Immediately Jesus stretched out his hand and caught him, and said to him, "O you of little faith, why did you doubt?"

Reflecting on the Word

"Lord, save me!" How often do we echo Peter's plea? It seems to burst forth when we feel overwhelmed, anxious, or drowning in responsibilities. Though Peter doubted and feared as much as we do sometimes, he also hoped in the Lord. He dared to come to Jesus, and when doubt caused him to sink, he reached out his hand and felt Jesus grab him tight. He was not left to drown in those turbulent waters, and neither are we. Jesus is there with a firm grasp; he alone can calm all our fears. Faith makes a difference in our lives. When we have faith, we respond courageously to adversity and unrest.

•••••• ON THE WAY TO MASS

Have you ever felt scared or worried? How did you get over these your fears and anxieties?

ON THE WAY HOME FROM MASS ••••••

How has Jesus been there for you in times of turmoil?

Living the Word

Jesus gave Peter his hand as Peter was falling into the water. Talk about what it means to "lend a helping hand." Who might benefit from a helping hand this week? Ask everyone in your family to lend a helping hand each day this week and to share their experiences at the dinner table.

August 16, 2020

Twentieth Sunday in Ordinary Time

Hearing the Word

Matthew 15:21–28

In the name of the Father, and of the Son, and of the Holy Spirit.

At that time, Jesus withdrew to the region of Tyre and Sidon. And behold, a Canaanite woman of that district came and called out, "Have pity on me, Lord, Son of David! My daughter is tormented by a demon." But Jesus did not say a word in answer to her. His disciples came and asked him, "Send her away, for she keeps calling out after us." He said in reply, "I was sent only to the lost sheep of the house of Israel." But the woman came and did Jesus homage, saying, "Lord, help me." He said in reply, "It is not right to take the food of the children and throw it to the dogs." She said, "Please, Lord, for even the dogs eat the scraps that fall from the table of their masters." Then Jesus said to her in reply, "O woman, great is your faith! Let it be done for you as you wish." And her daughter was healed from that hour.

Reflecting on the Word

Today, we hear another story of the power of faith. When the Canaanite woman asks for healing for her daughter, Jesus tells her it is not right to take the food of the children and throw it to the dogs. But, she points out that she does not need to *take* the food—even the scraps will be enough. We, the baptized, are invited to the feast at Christ's table. The food is so rich, that even one crumb would be enough.

• • • • • • ON THE WAY TO MASS

Ask your family to pay attention to the moment at Mass when we say, "Lord, I am not worthy that you should enter under my roof, but only say the word and my soul shall be healed."

ON THE WAY HOME FROM MASS • • • • • •

What do the words said before receiving Holy Communion mean in light of today's Gospel?

Living the Word

God always hears what we ask, in prayer, and gives us the healing we need. At home, read the Gospel passage on the previous page aloud to your children. Ask them to imagine that the woman followed Jesus for two hours, begging him to heal her daughter. Sometimes in life, we have to be as focused and persistent as this woman was with Jesus. We must have a persistent faith in God.

Twenty-First Sunday in Ordinary Time

Hearing the Word

Matthew 16:15–18

In the name of the Father, and of the Son, and of the Holy Spirit.

[Jesus said to his disciples:] "But who do you say that I am?" Simon Peter said in reply, "You are the Christ, the Son of the living God." Jesus said to him in reply, "Blessed are you, Simon son of Jonah. For flesh and blood has not revealed this to you, but my heavenly Father. And so I say to you, you are Peter, and upon this rock I will build my church, and the gates of the netherworld shall not prevail against it."

Reflecting on the Word

If we, with Peter, profess that Jesus is the Son of the living God, then our lives must change. If we truly believe that God has sacrificed everything, even life, out of love for us, then we who are made in the image and likeness of God are called to do the same. That radical love can hurt; it will upset our lives and make us less comfortable. But when we love as Christ loves, we build up his Church. In daring to proclaim who Jesus is, we also profess our own selves: Who am I? Who am I called to be?

● ● ● ● ● ● ON THE WAY TO MASS

Ask your children to relate what they already know about St. Peter. Let them know that in today's Gospel, Peter will be entrusted with the care of the Church because of how he responds to Jesus' question.

ON THE WAY HOME FROM MASS ● ● ● ● ● ●

St. Peter is the Church's first pope. He was graced with the recognition that Jesus is the Christ. Who is our current pope? How does he continue Jesus' work today?

Living the Word

In 2016, Pope Francis wrote *Amoris laetitia* to advise the Church on how to care for families. He reflects deeply on the meaning of love in the day-to-day reality of family life. Discuss with your spouse how you are raising your children to be Christians. How does our family teach Christian values? How do we teach them to be sensitive to others' sufferings?

August 30, 2020

Twenty-Second Sunday in Ordinary Time

Hearing the Word
Matthew 16:21–25

In the name of the Father, and of the Son, and of the Holy Spirit.

Jesus began to show his disciples that he must go to Jerusalem and suffer greatly from the elders, the chief priests, and the scribes, and be killed and on the third day be raised. Then Peter took Jesus aside and began to rebuke him, "God forbid, Lord! No such thing shall ever happen to you." He turned and said to Peter, "Get behind me, Satan! You are an obstacle to me. You are thinking not as God does, but as human beings do."

Then Jesus said to his disciples, "Whoever wishes to come after me must deny himself, take up his cross, and follow me. For whoever wishes to save his life will lose it, but whoever loses his life for my sake will find it."

Reflecting on the Word

Peter responded to Jesus as any of us might: "God forbid anything bad would happen!" And just like that, Peter, the rock of the church, became a stumbling block. He failed to see with God's eyes, to accept the logic of the Cross, which is that God would heal through death, bring peace from violence and offer hope from suffering. We cannot avoid pain and disappointment. Instead, we are called to lay down our expectations and desires and take up our burdens with hope.

......ON THE WAY TO MASS

What does it mean to suffer? Is all suffering good or bad?

ON THE WAY HOME FROM MASS ......

Talk with your children about being empathetic to the suffering of others. (You might refer to last week's conversation you and your spouse had about raising your children as Christians.) How might we respond when we see others who are sad or in pain?

Living the Word

Discuss what Jesus means when he says to "take up your cross." What is your cross? How do you take it up? Why do you think this is how we follow Jesus? Sing or listen to the hymn "Take Up Your Cross." Encourage all family members to wear or keep a cross with them for the whole week as a reminder of Jesus' words.

EVERYDAY
FAMILY PRAYERS

The Sign of the Cross

The Sign of the Cross is the first prayer and the last: of each day, and of each Christian life. It is a prayer of the body as well as a prayer of words. When we are presented for Baptism, the community traces this sign on our bodies for the first time. Parents may trace it daily on their children. We learn to trace it daily on ourselves and on those whom we love. When we die, our loved ones will trace this holy sign on us for the last time.

In the name of the Father,

and of the Son,

and of the Holy Spirit. Amen.

The Lord's Prayer

The Lord's Prayer, or the Our Father, is a very important prayer for Christians because Jesus himself taught it to his disciples, who taught it to his Church. Today, we say this prayer as part of Mass, in the Rosary, and in personal prayer. There are seven petitions in the Lord's Prayer. The first three ask for God to be glorified and praised, and the next four ask for God to help take care of our physical and spiritual needs.

Our Father, who art in heaven,

hallowed be thy name;

thy kingdom come,

thy will be done

on earth as it is in heaven.

Give us this day our daily bread,

and forgive us our trespasses,

as we forgive those who trespass against us;

and lead us not into temptation, but deliver us from evil.

The Apostles' Creed

The Apostles' Creed is one of the earliest creeds we have; scholars believe it was written within the second century. The Apostles' Creed is shorter than the Nicene Creed, but it states what we believe about the Father, Son, and Holy Spirit. This prayer is sometimes used at Mass, especially at Masses with children, and is part of the Rosary.

I believe in God,

the Father almighty,

Creator of heaven and earth,

and in Jesus Christ, his only Son, our Lord,

who was conceived by the Holy Spirit,

born of the Virgin Mary,

suffered under Pontius Pilate,

was crucified, died and was buried;

he descended into hell;

and on the third day he rose again from the dead;

he ascended into heaven,

and is seated at the right hand of God the Father almighty;

from there he will come to judge the living and the dead.

I believe in the Holy Spirit,

the holy catholic Church,

the communion of saints,

the forgiveness of sins,

the resurrection of the body,

and life everlasting. Amen.

The Nicene Creed

The Nicene Creed was written at the Council of Nicaea in AD 325, when bishops of the Church gathered together in order to articulate true belief in who Christ is and in his relationship to God the Father. The Nicene Creed was the final document of that Council, written so that all the faithful may know the central teachings of Christianity. We say this prayer at Mass.

I believe in one God,

the Father almighty,

maker of heaven and earth,

of all things visible and invisible.

I believe in one Lord Jesus Christ,

the Only Begotten Son of God,

born of the Father before all ages.

God from God, Light from Light,

true God from true God,

begotten, not made, consubstantial with the Father;

through him all things were made.

For us men and for our salvation

he came down from heaven,

and by the Holy Spirit was incarnate of the Virgin Mary,

and became man.

For our sake he was crucified under Pontius Pilate,

he suffered death and was buried,

and rose again on the third day

in accordance with the Scriptures.
He ascended into heaven
and is seated at the right hand of the Father.
He will come again in glory
to judge the living and the dead
and his kingdom will have no end.

I believe in the Holy Spirit, the Lord, the giver of life,
who proceeds from the Father and the Son,
who with the Father and Son is adored and glorified,
who has spoken through the prophets.

I believe in one holy, catholic, and apostolic Church.
I confess one Baptism for the forgiveness of sins
and I look forward to the resurrection of the dead
and the life of the world to come. Amen.

Glory Be (Doxology)

This is a short prayer that Christians sometimes add to the end of psalms. It is prayed during the Rosary and usually follows the opening verse during the Liturgy of the Hours. It can be prayed at any time during the day.

Glory be to the Father

and to the Son

and to the Holy Spirit,

as it was in the beginning

is now, and ever shall be

world without end. Amen.

Hail Mary

The first two lines of this prayer are the words of the angel Gabriel to Mary, when he announces that she is with child (Luke 1:28). The second two lines are Elizabeth's greeting to Mary (Luke 1:42). The last four lines come to us from deep in history, from where and from whom we do not know. This prayer is part of the Rosary and is often used by Christians for personal prayer.

Hail, Mary, full of grace,

the Lord is with thee.

Blessed art thou among women

and blessed is the fruit of thy womb, Jesus.

Holy Mary, Mother of God,

pray for us sinners,

now and at the hour of our death.

Amen.

Grace before Meals

Families pray before meals in different ways. Some families make up a prayer in their own words, other families sing a prayer, and many families use this traditional formula. Teach your children to say this prayer while signing themselves with the cross.

Bless us, O Lord, and these thy gifts,

which we are about to receive from thy bounty,

through Christ our Lord.

Amen.

Grace after Meals

Teach your children to say this prayer after meals, while signing themselves with the cross. The part in brackets is optional.

We give thee thanks, for all thy benefits,

almighty God, who lives and reigns forever.

[And may the souls of the faithful departed,

through the mercy of God, rest in peace.]

Amen.